I0497829

This coloring book Belongs to

....

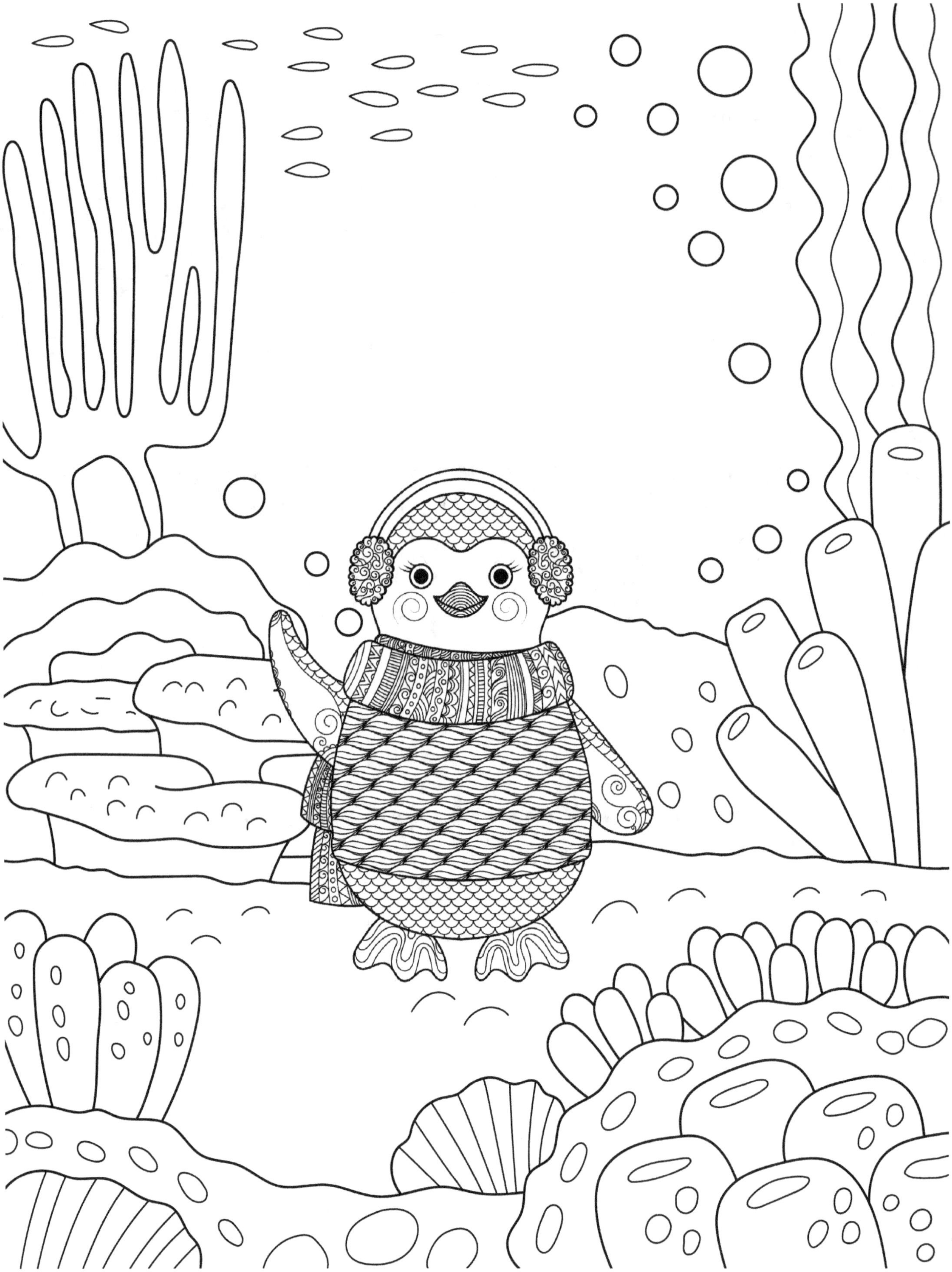

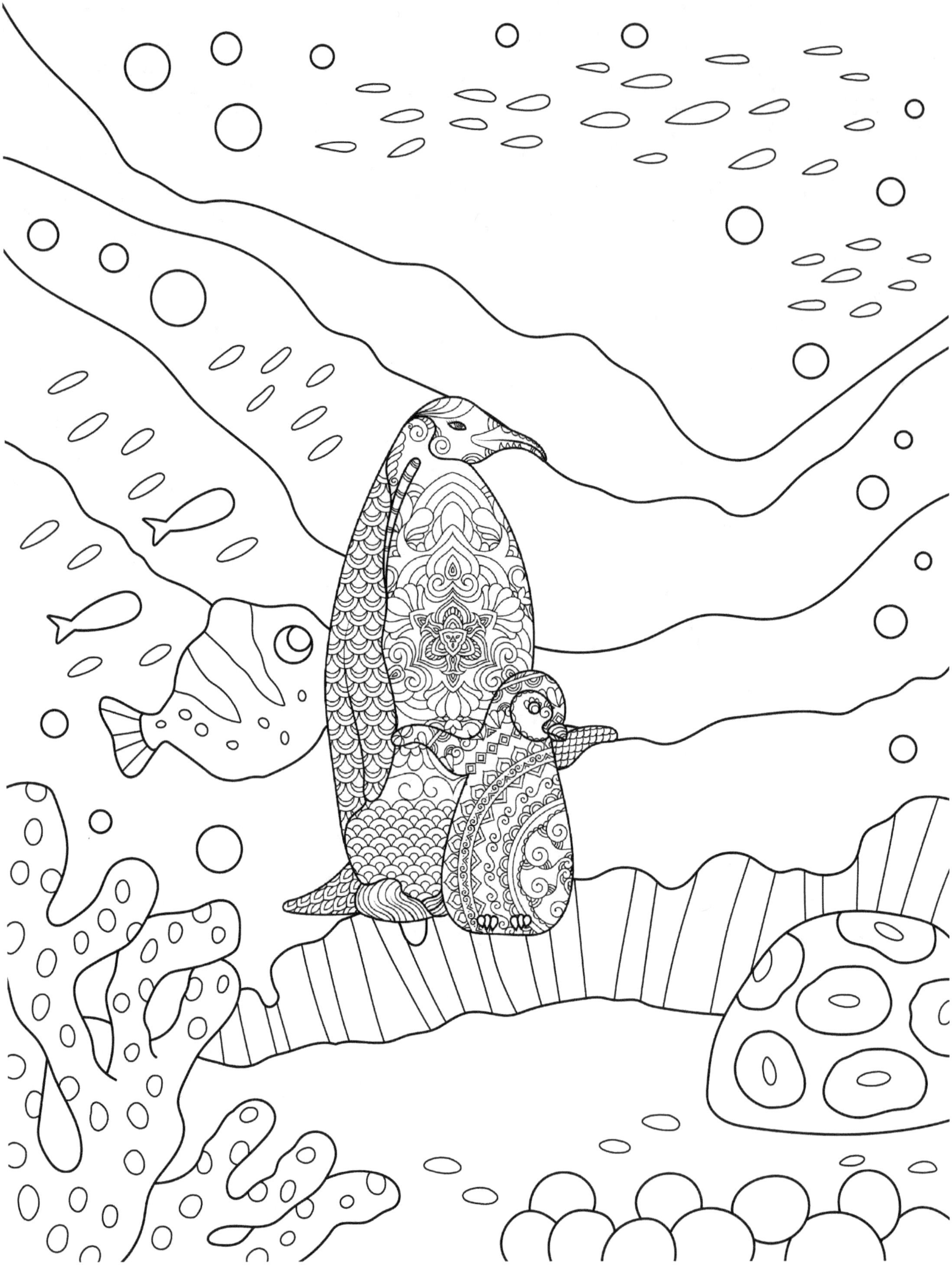

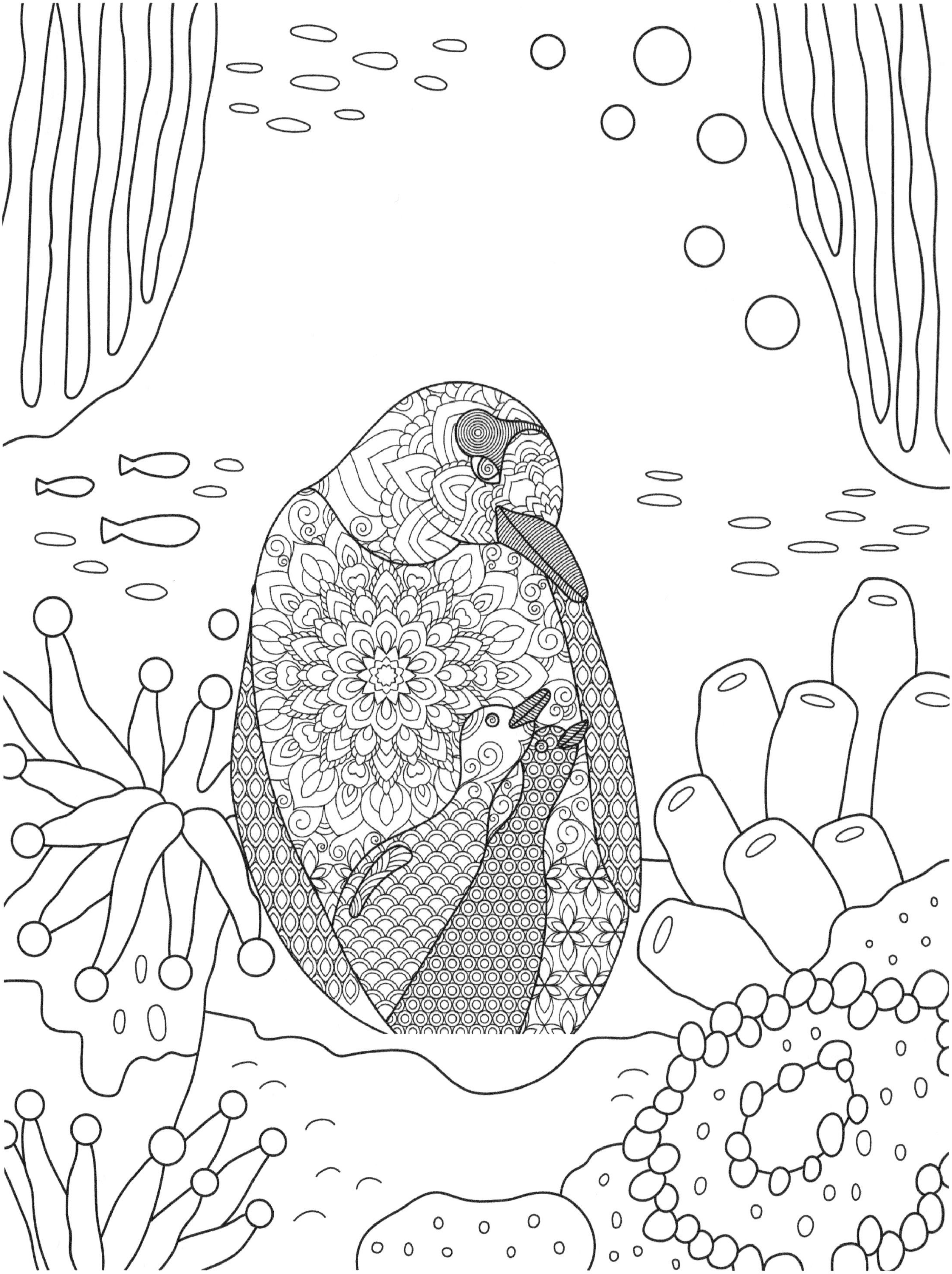

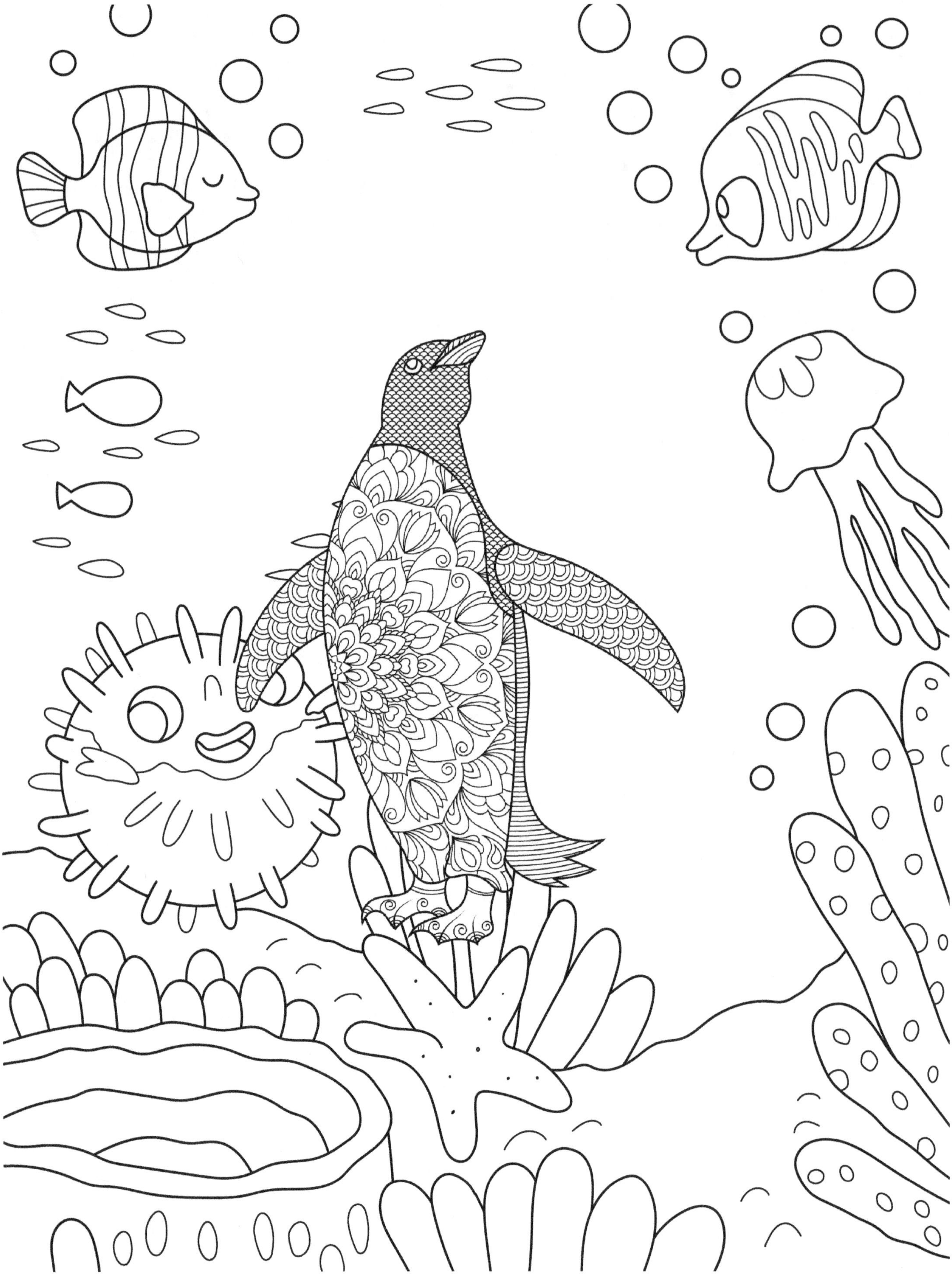

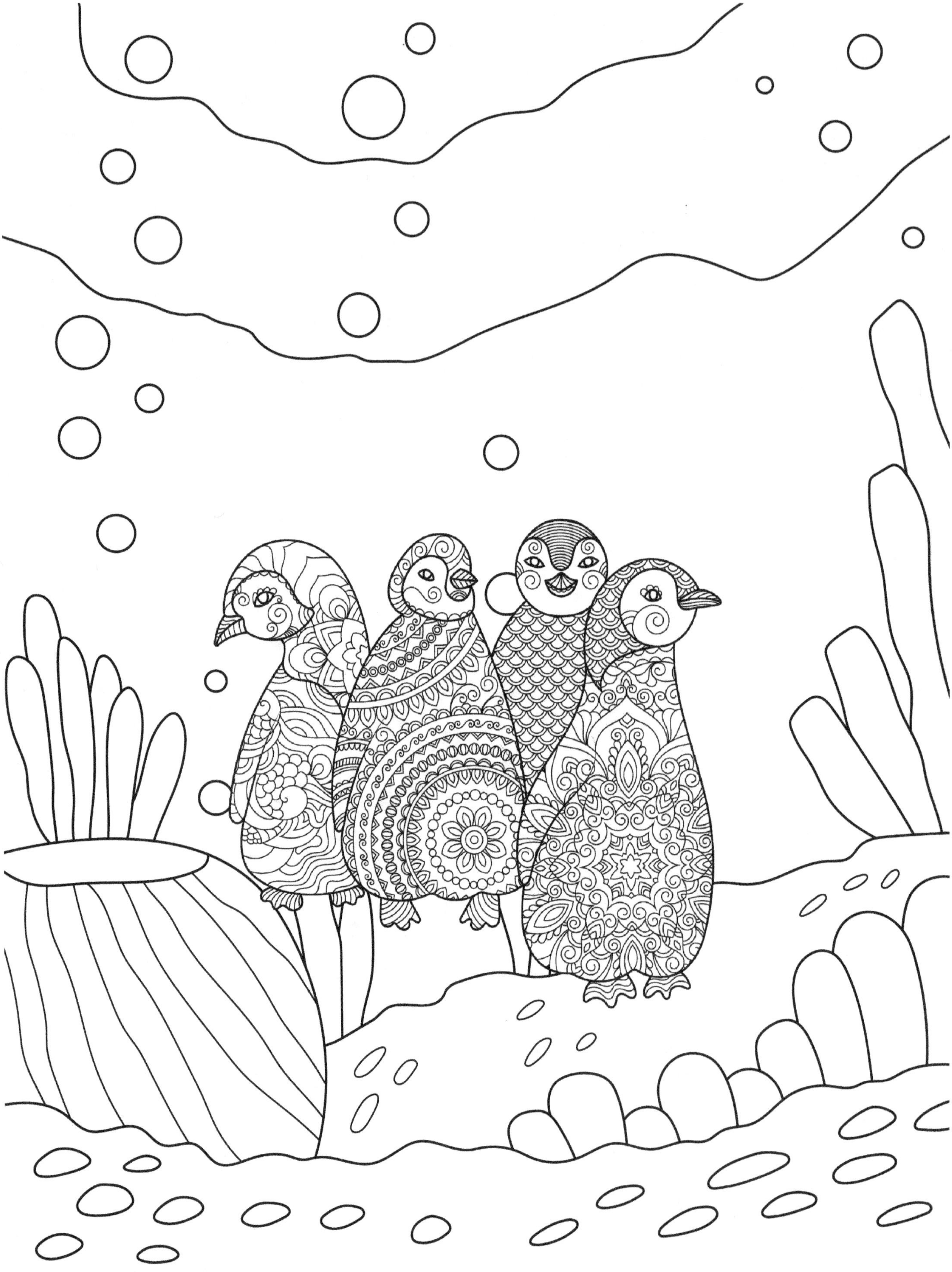

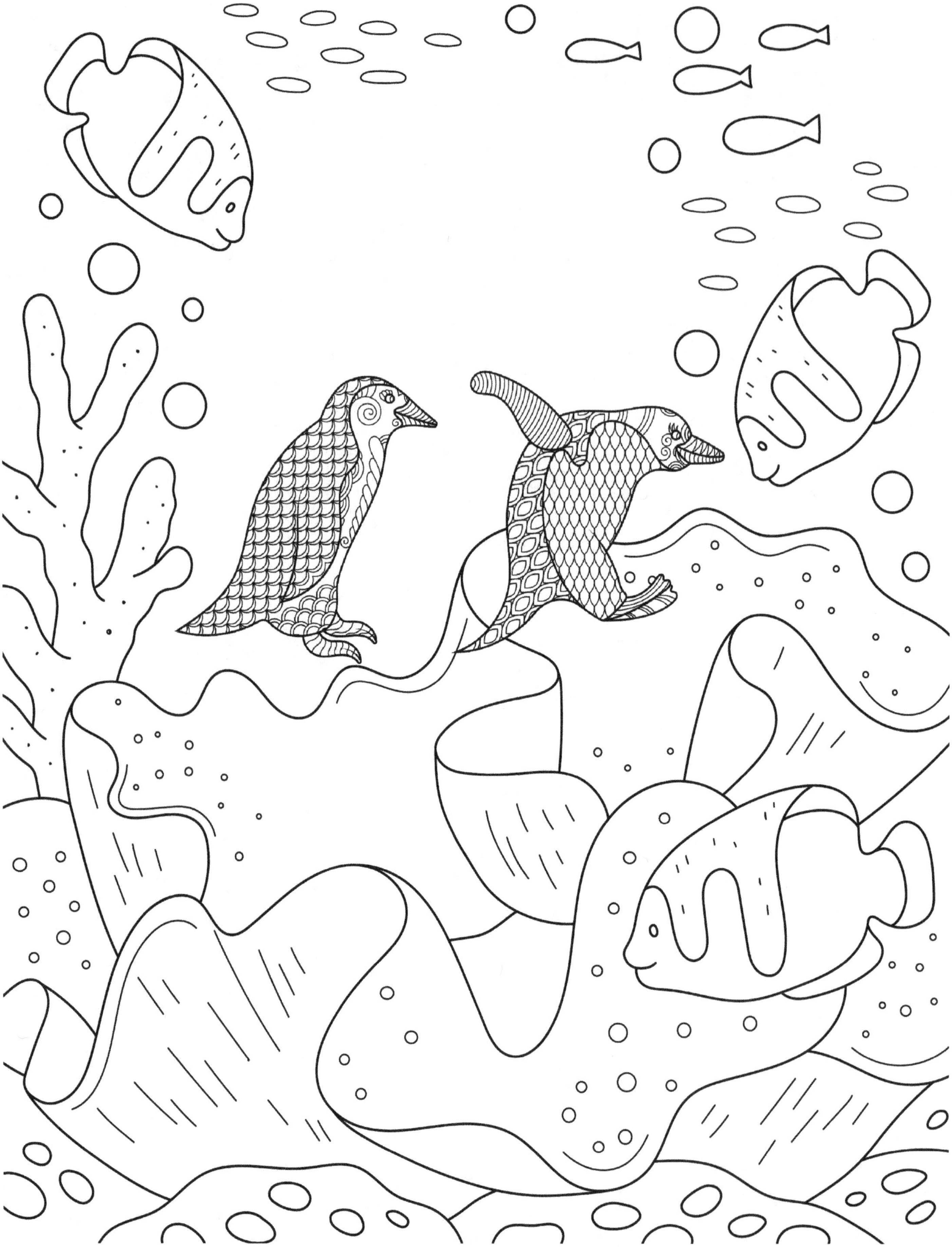

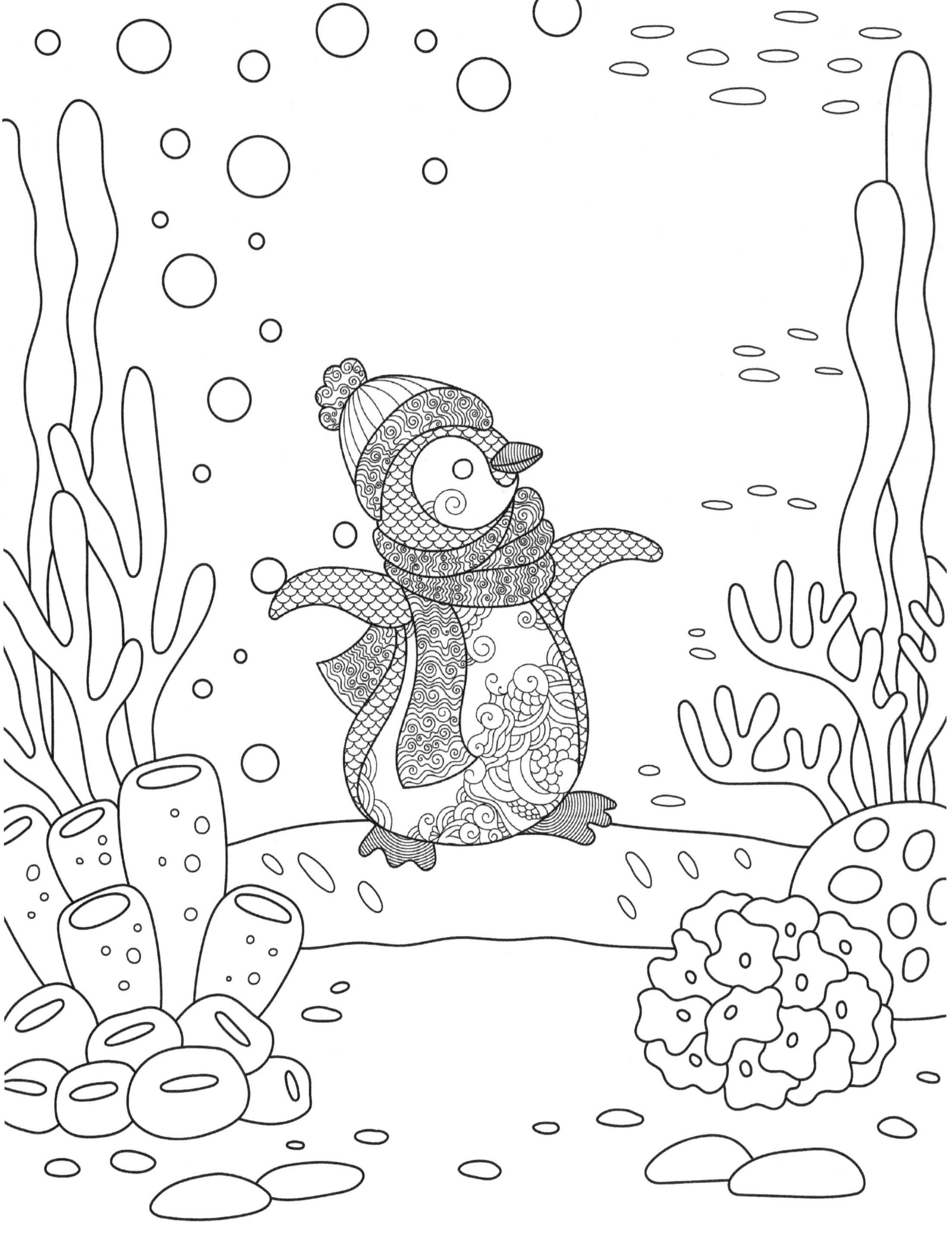

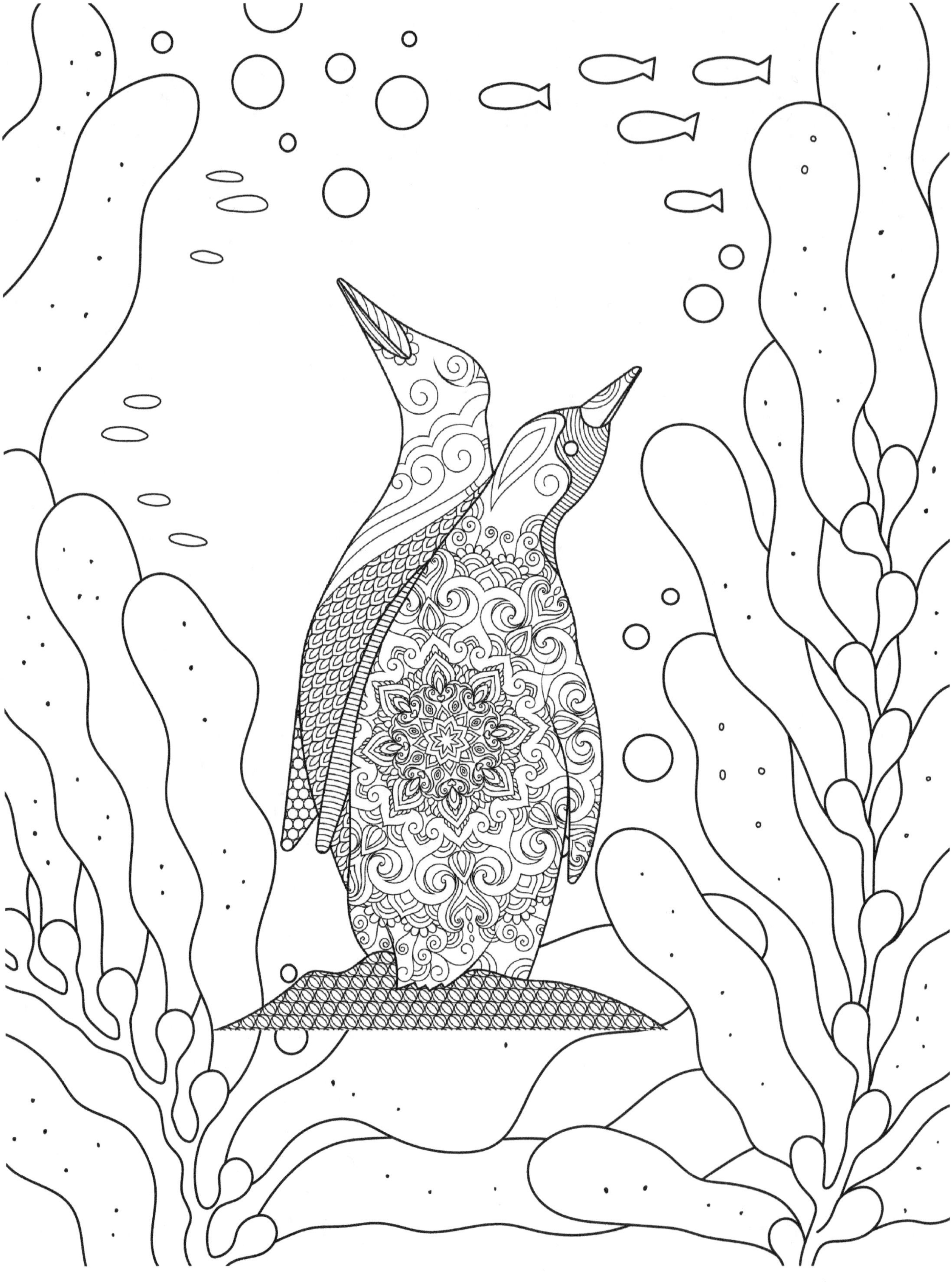

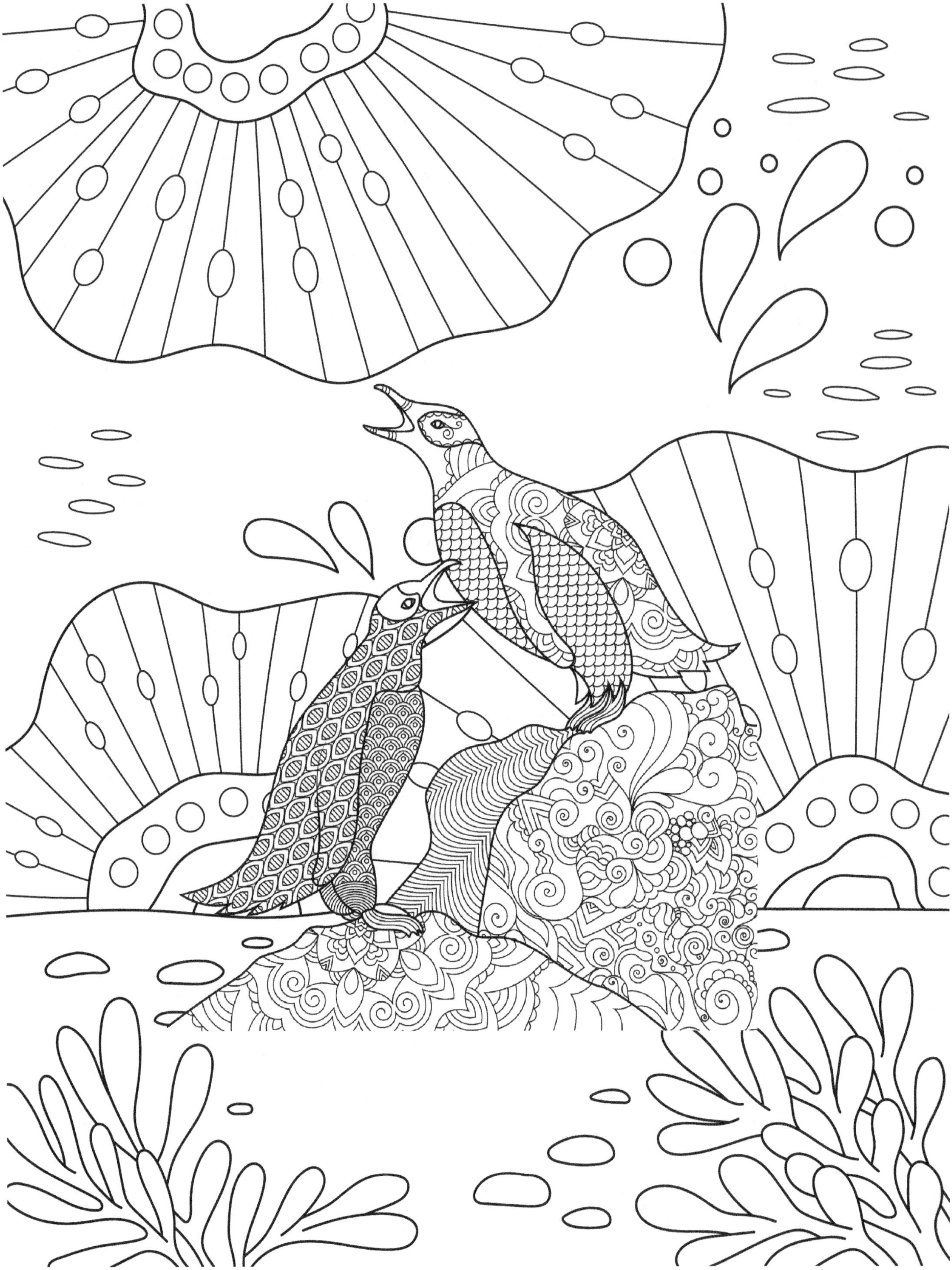

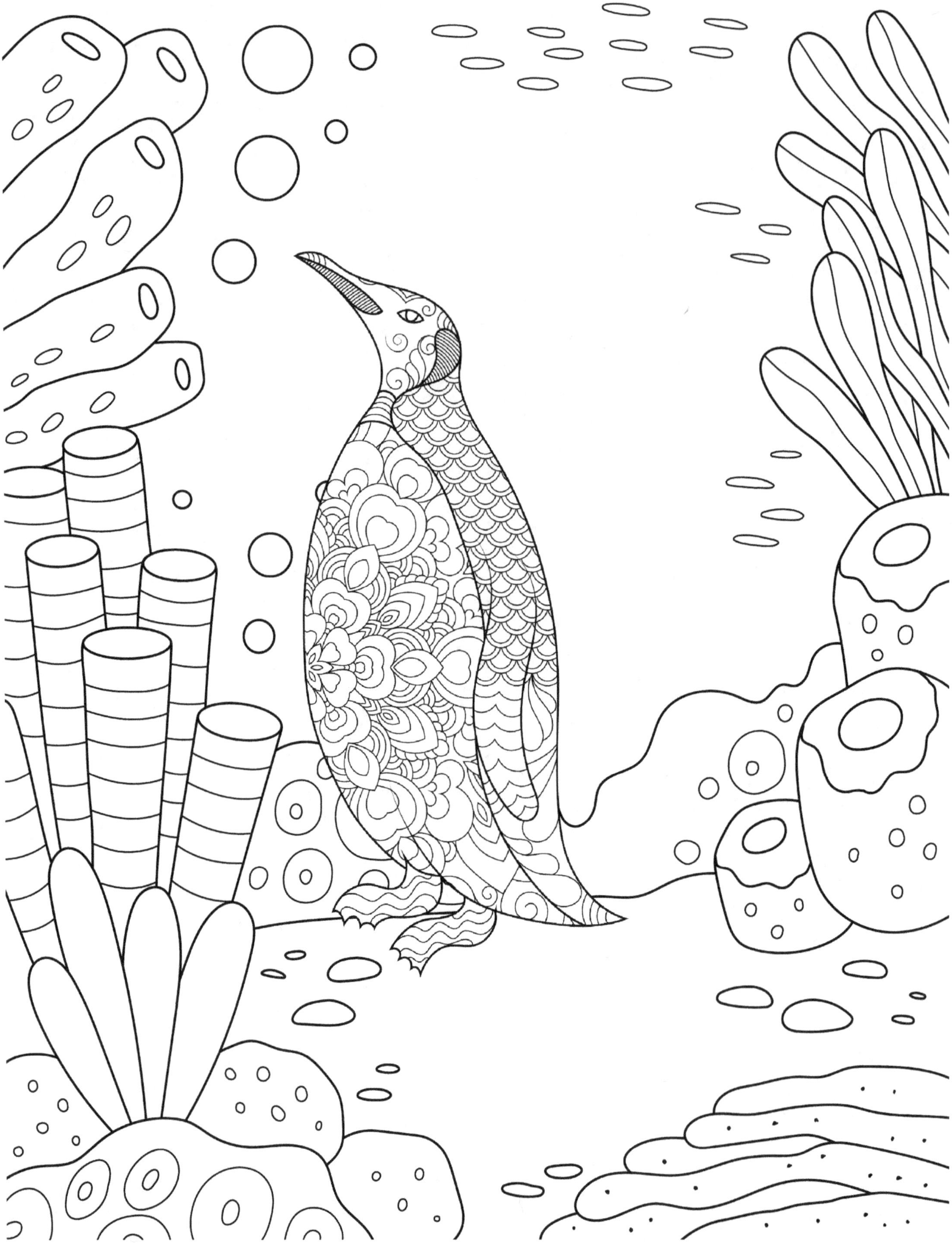

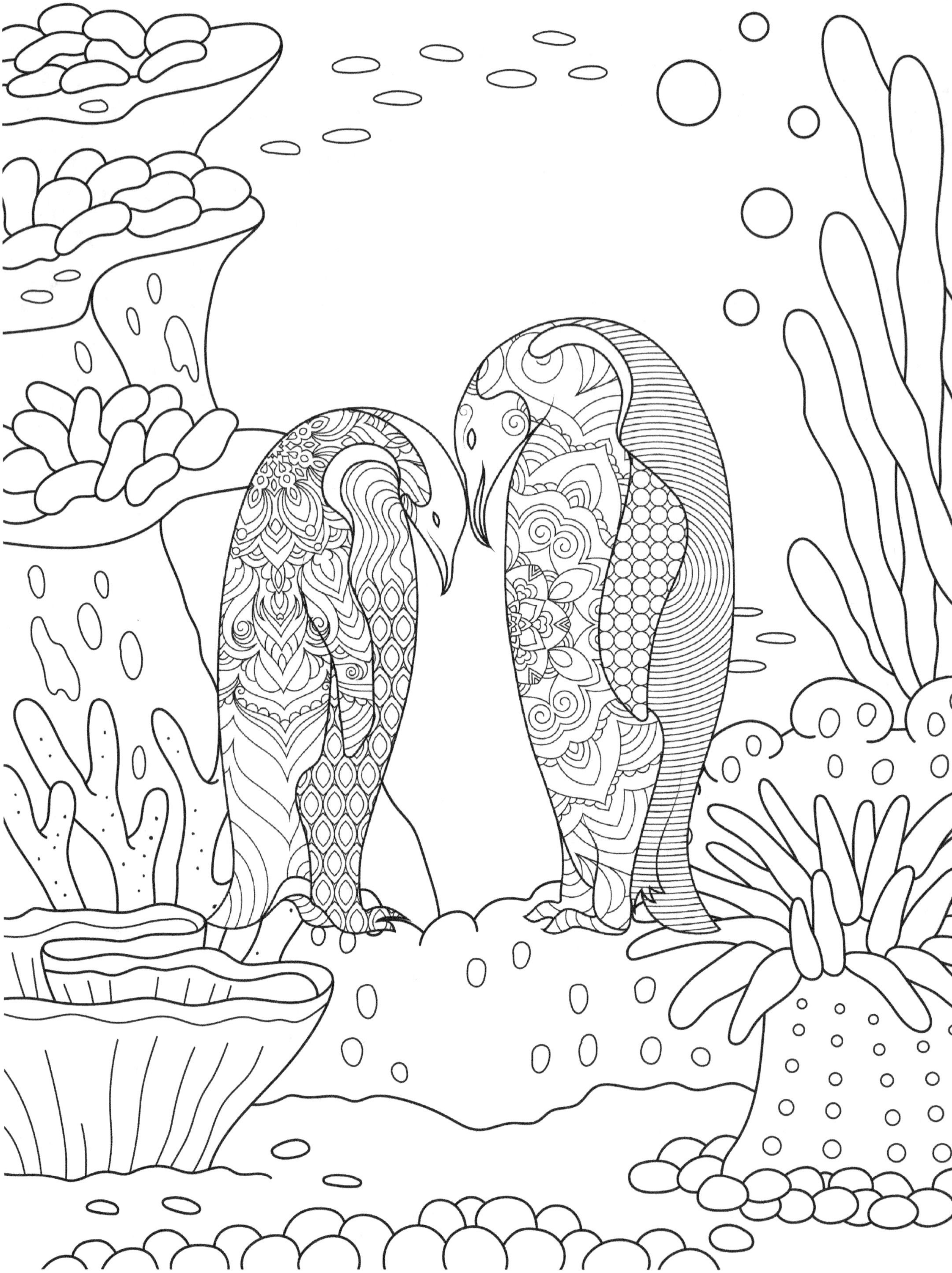

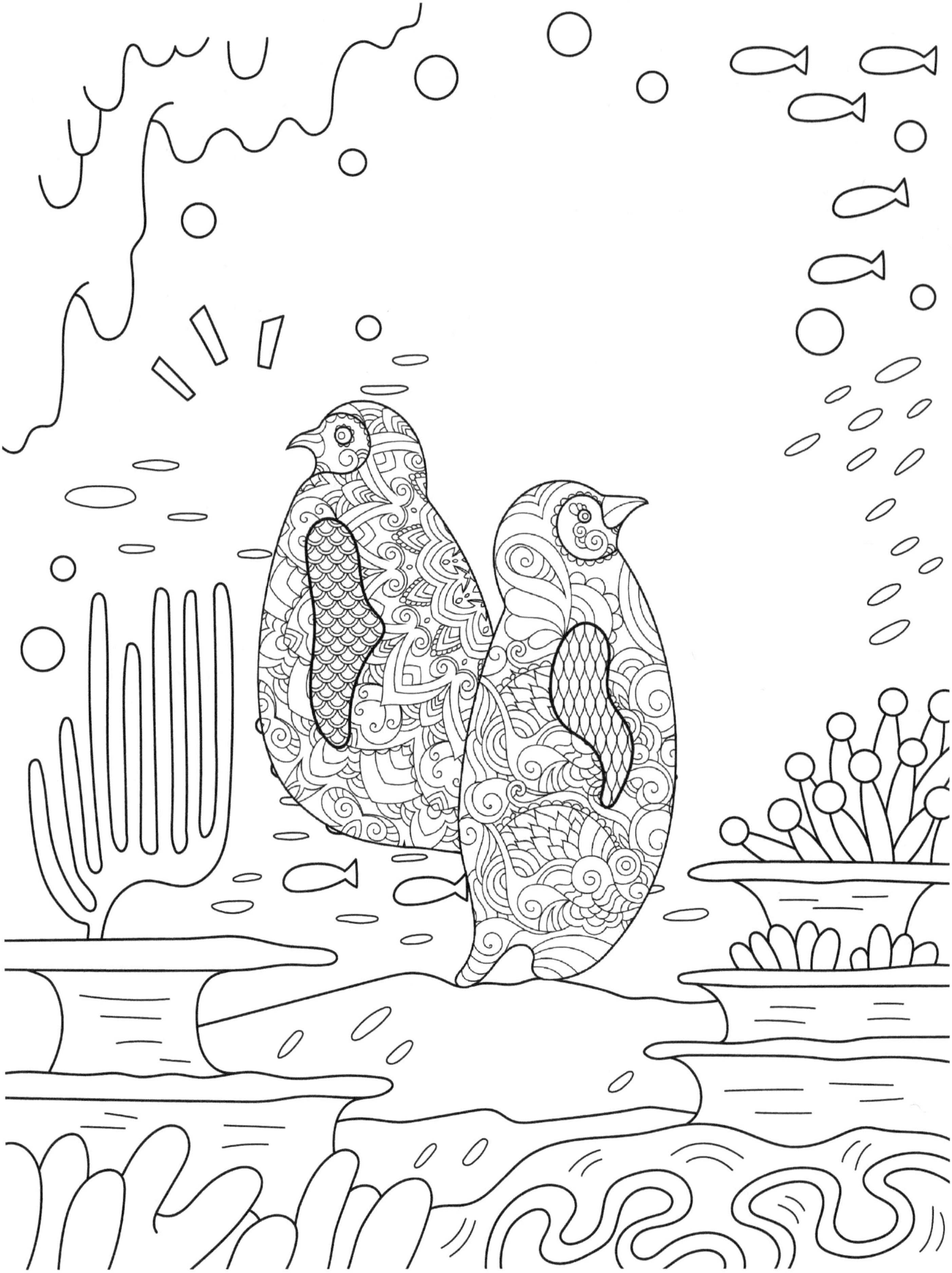

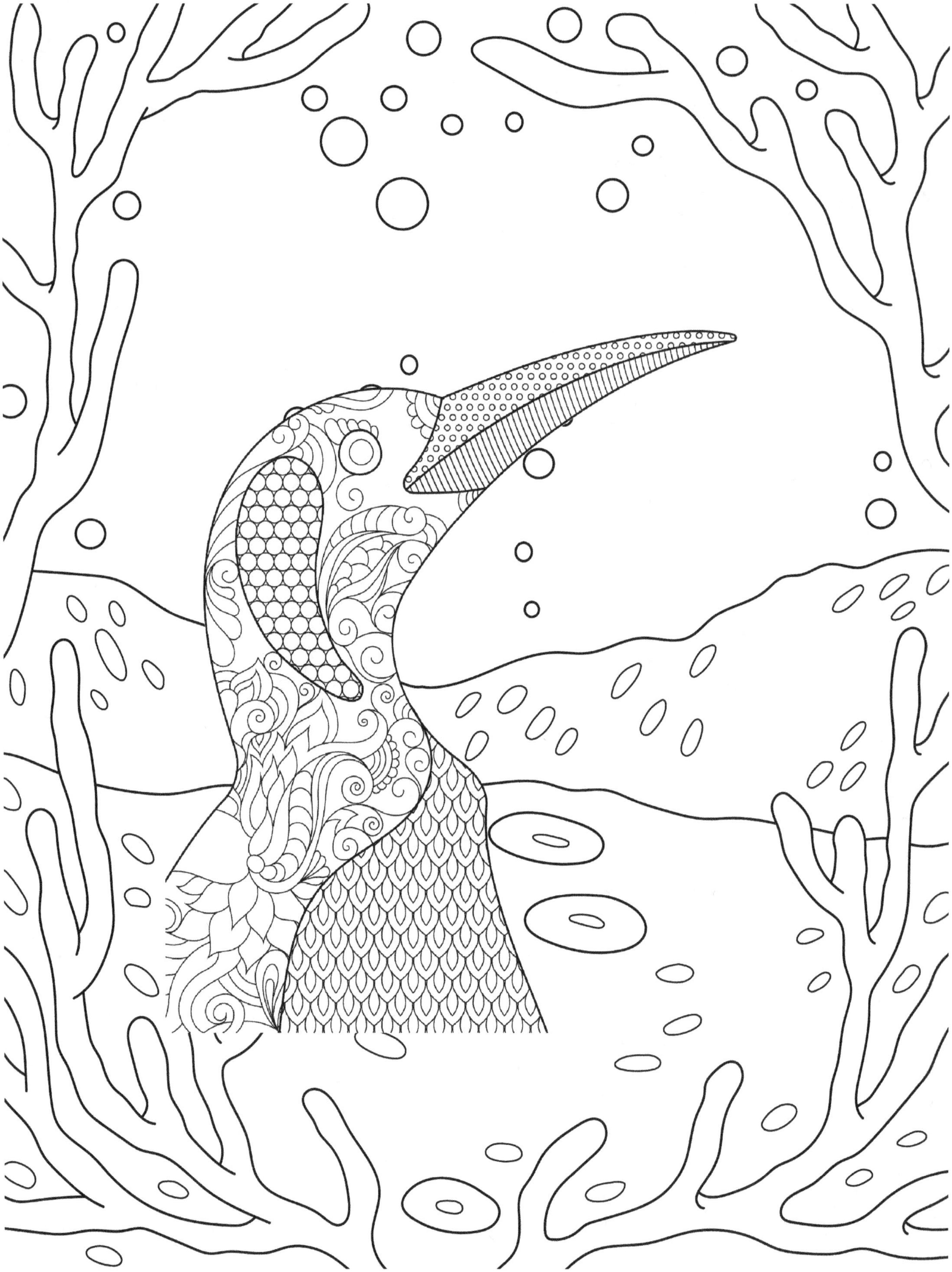

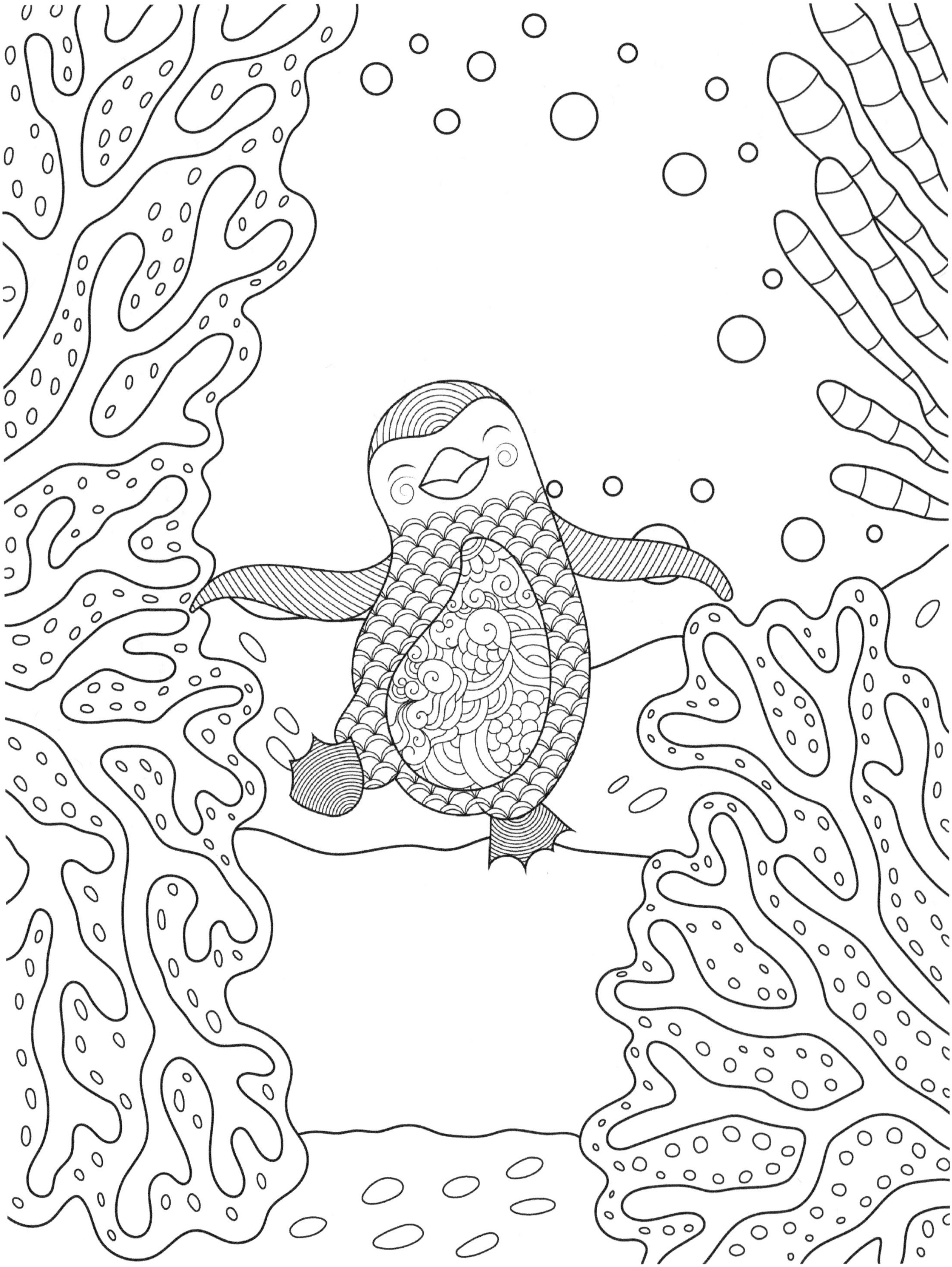

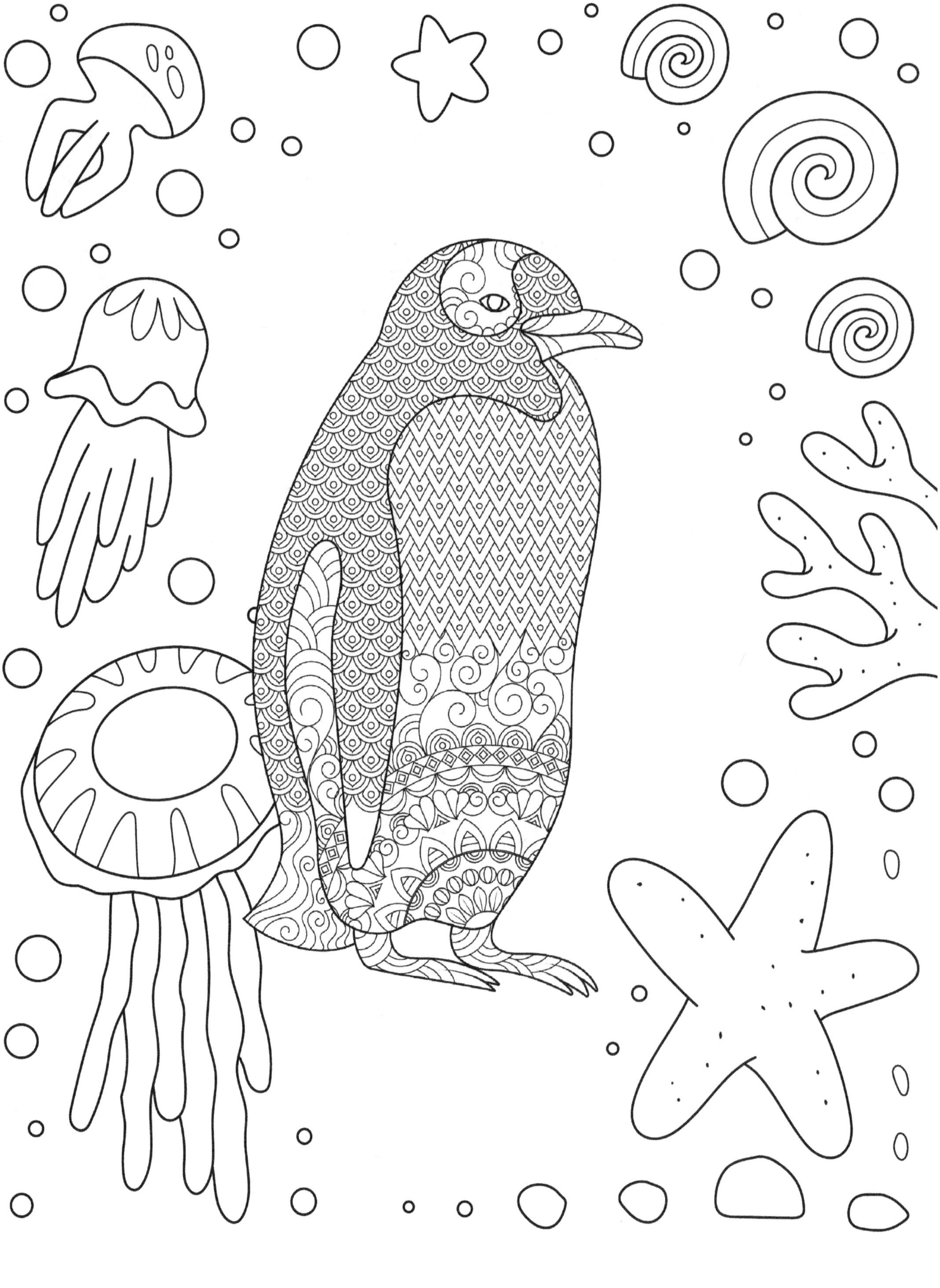

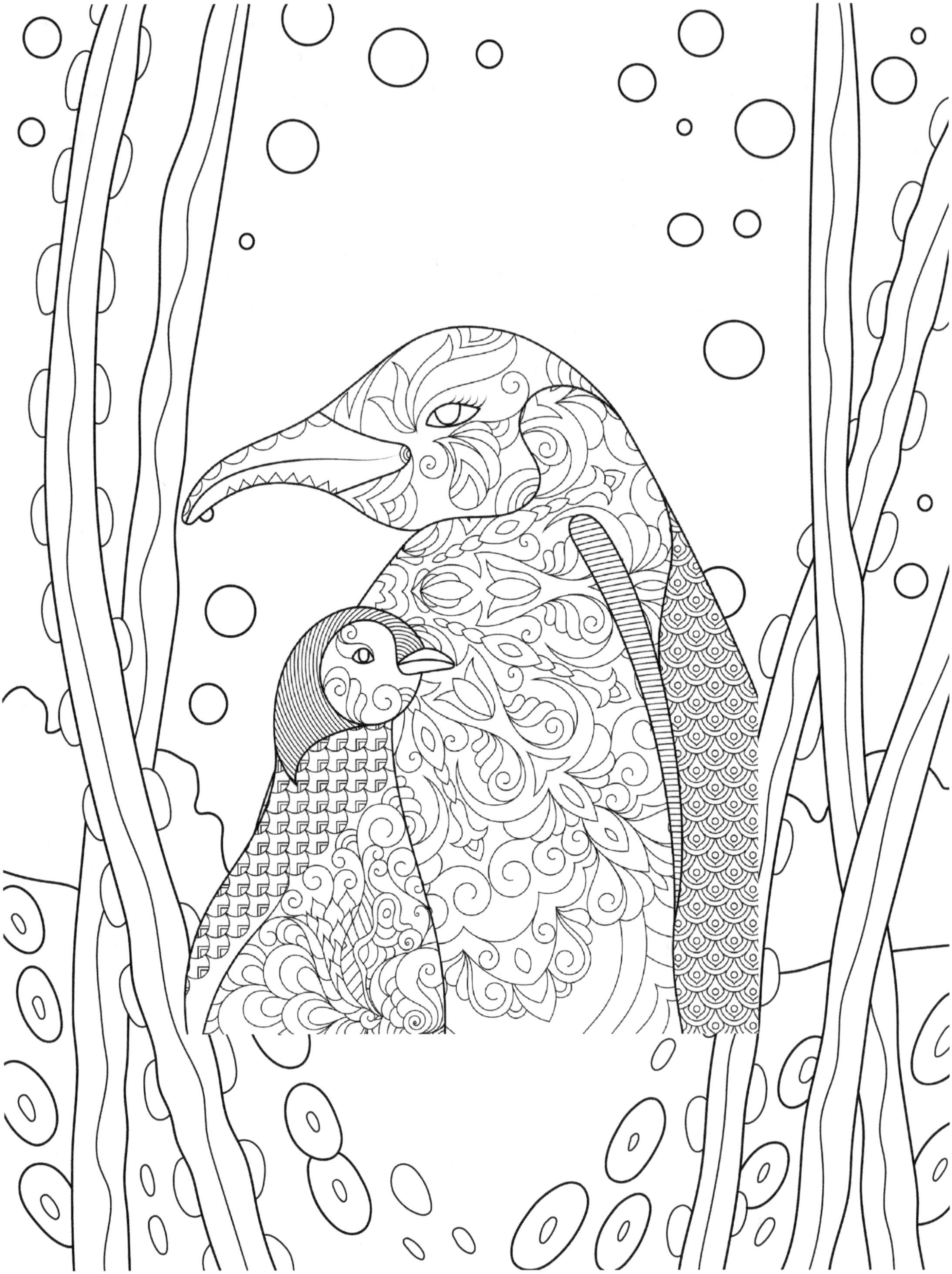

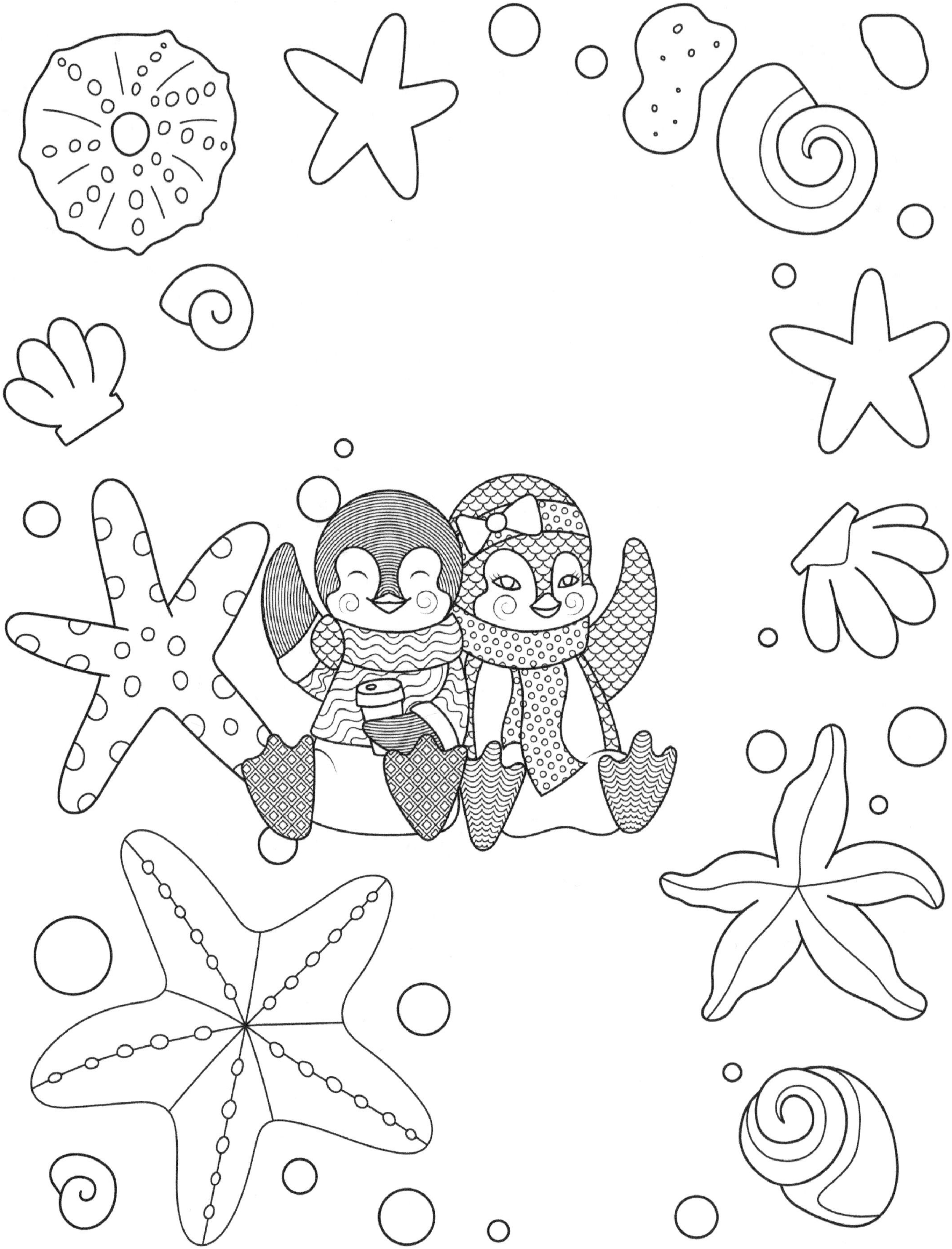

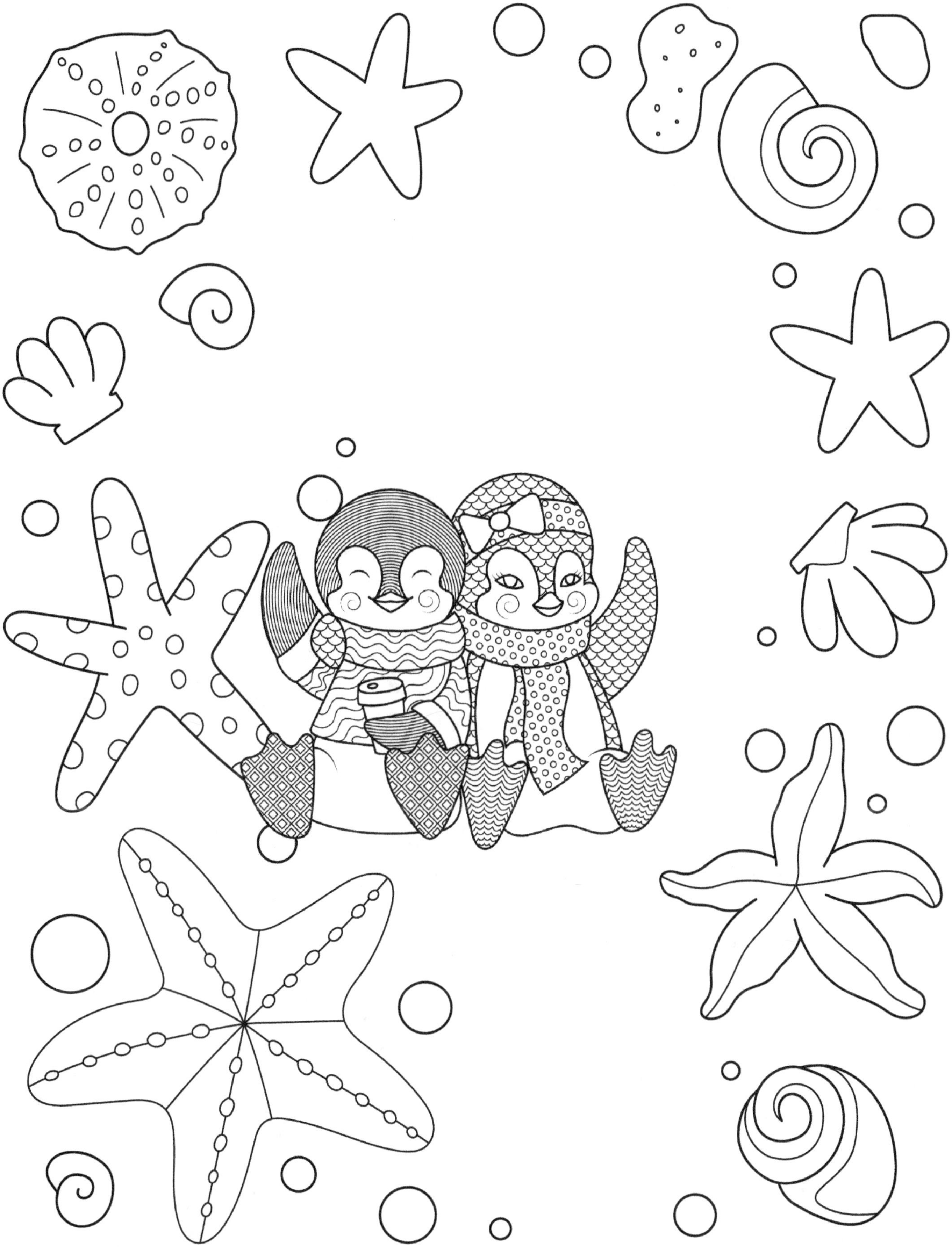

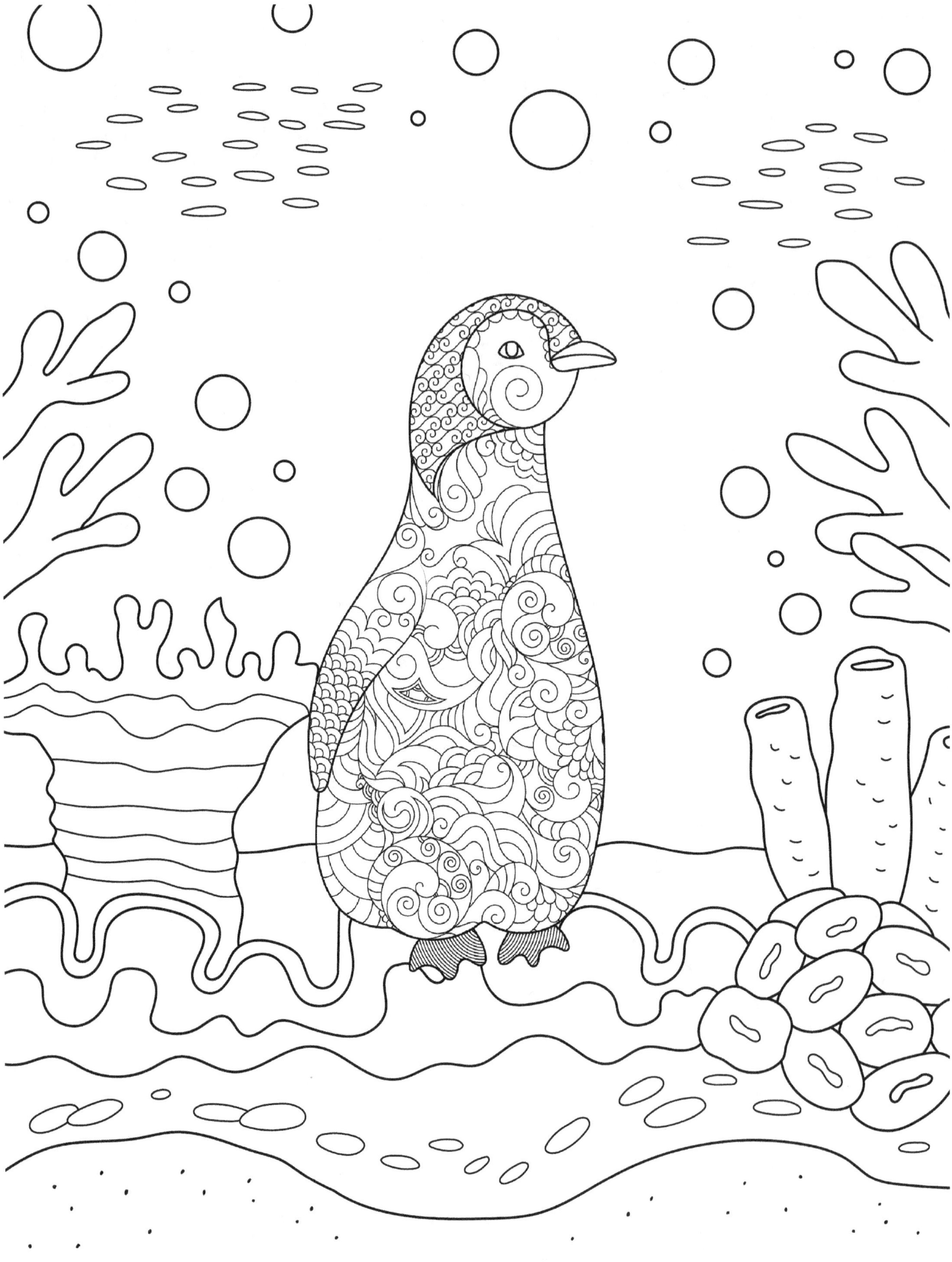

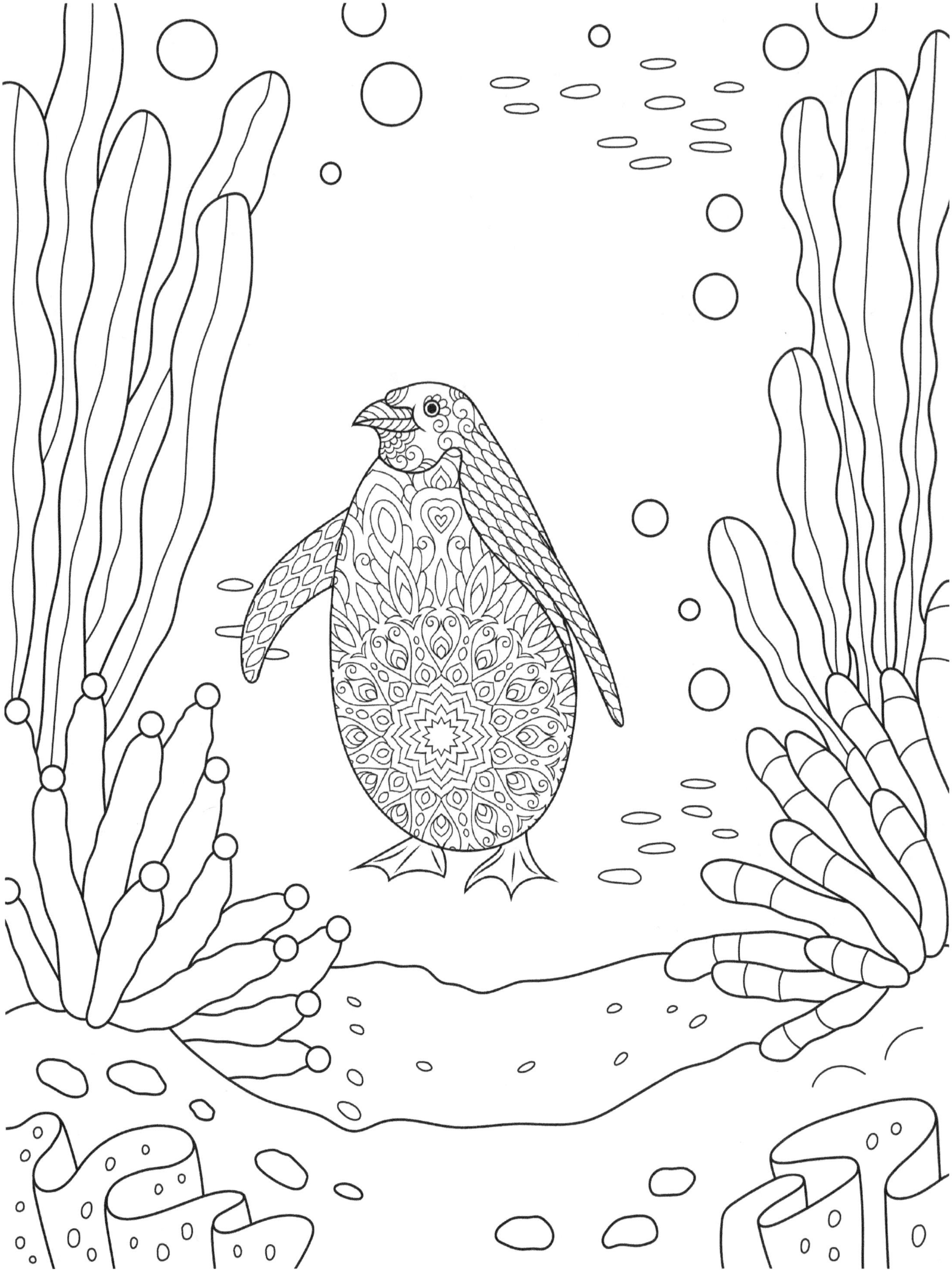

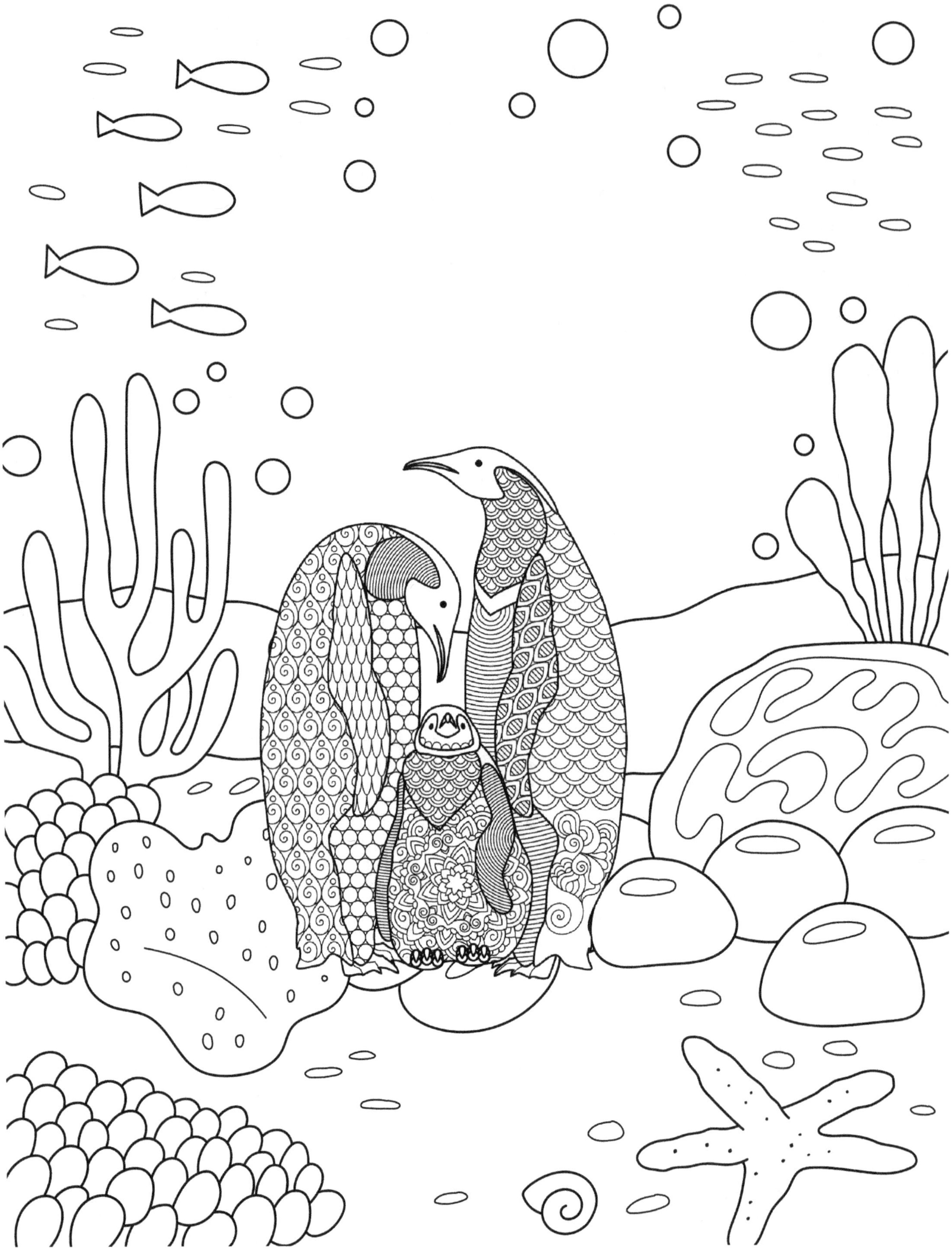

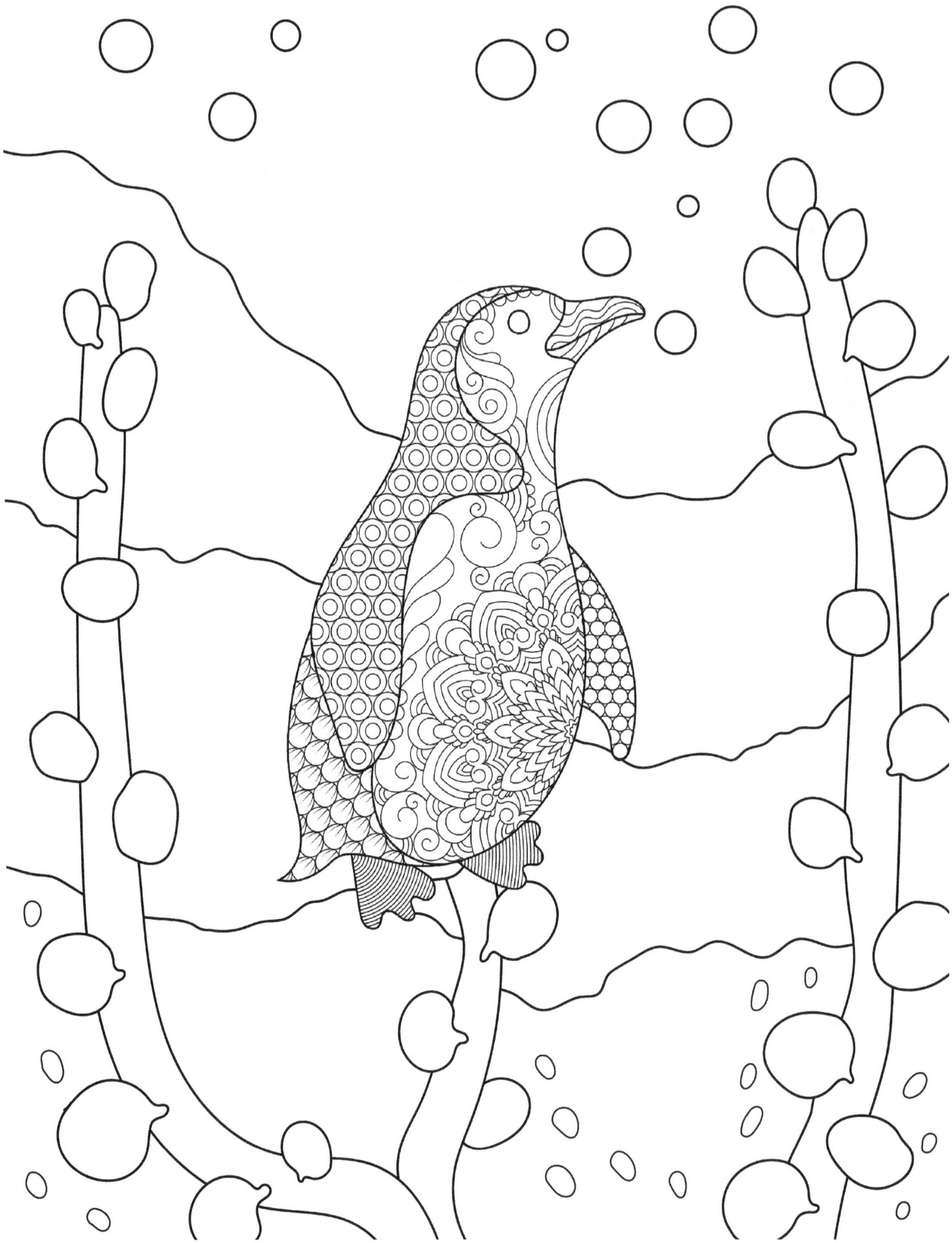

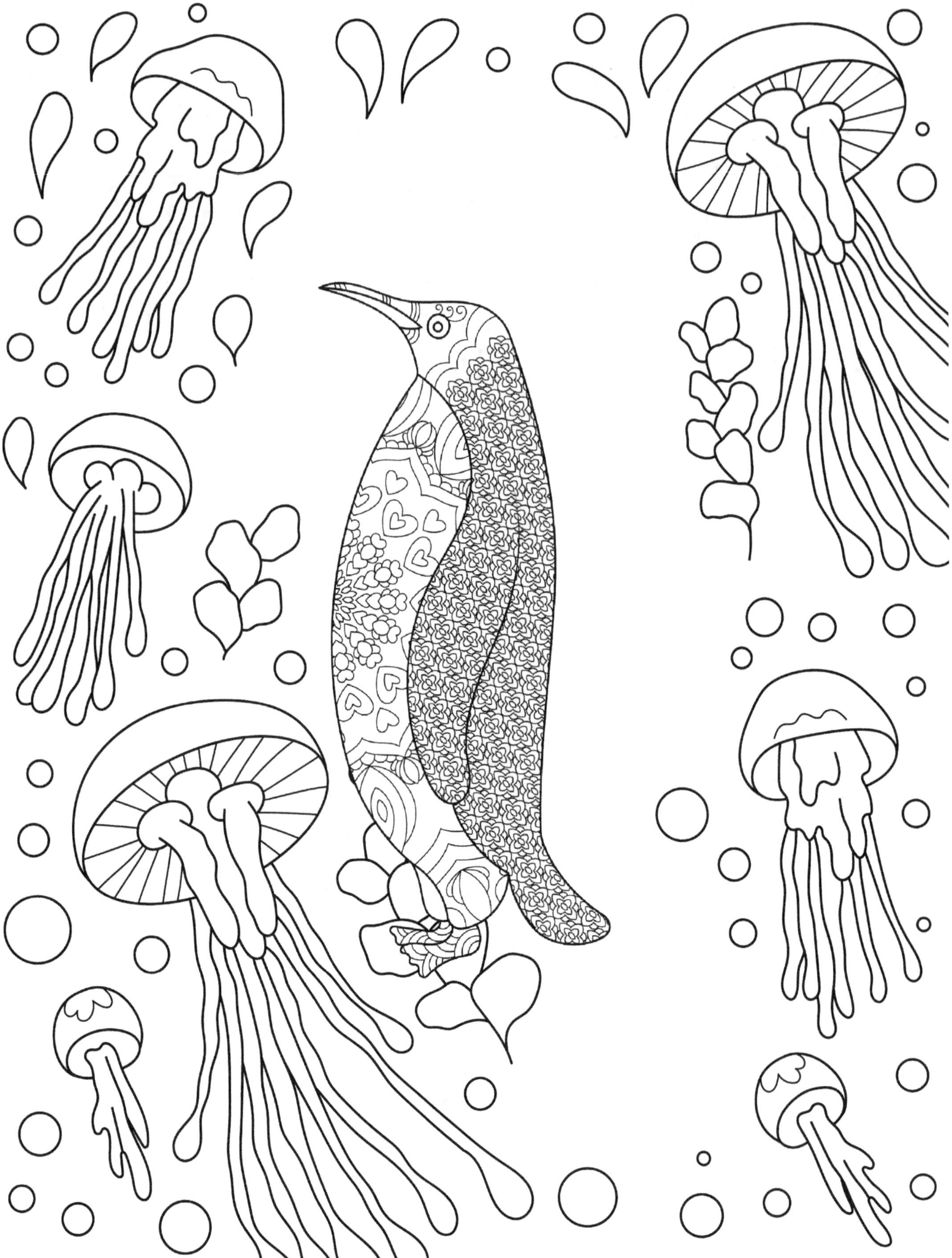

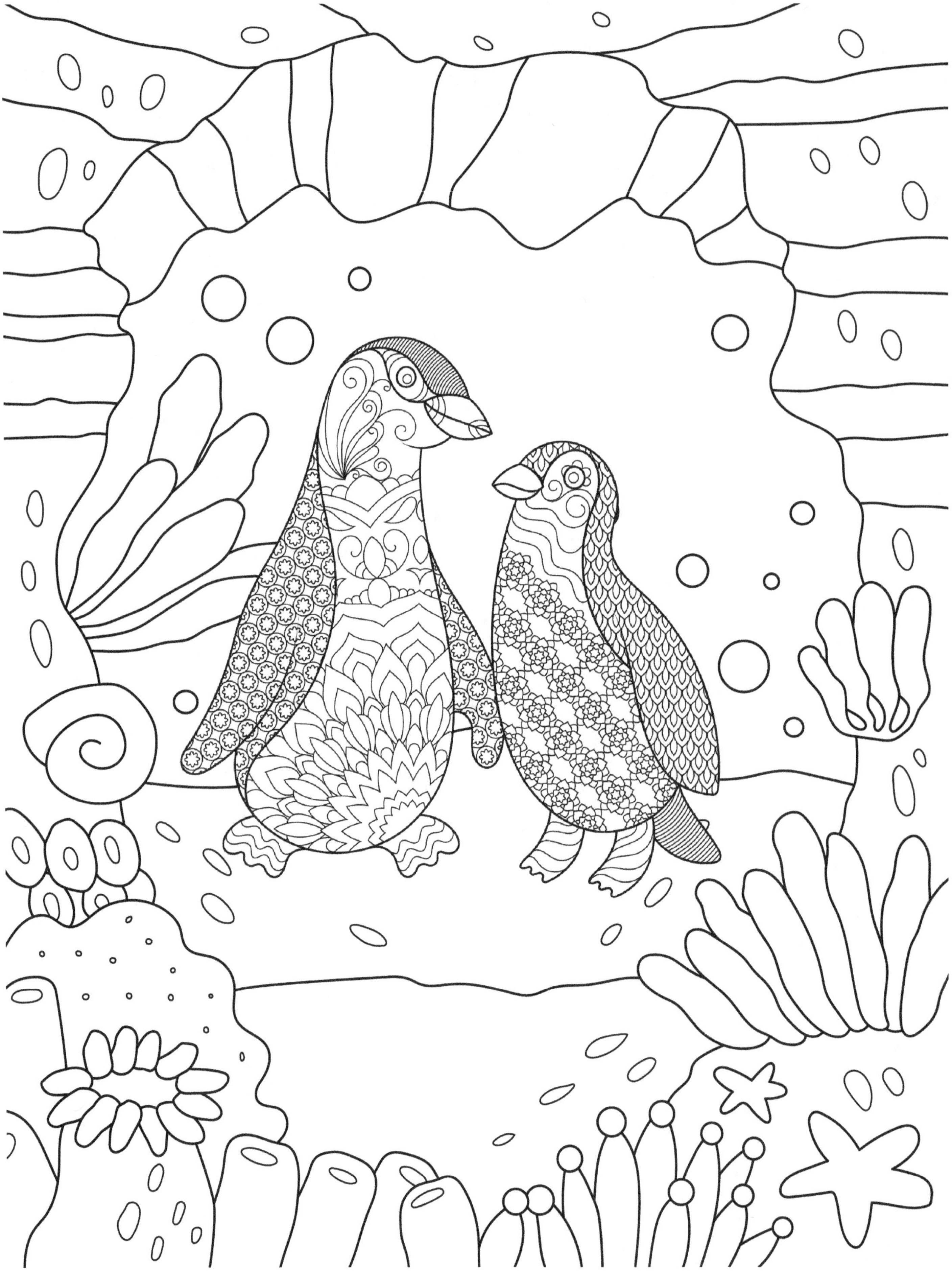

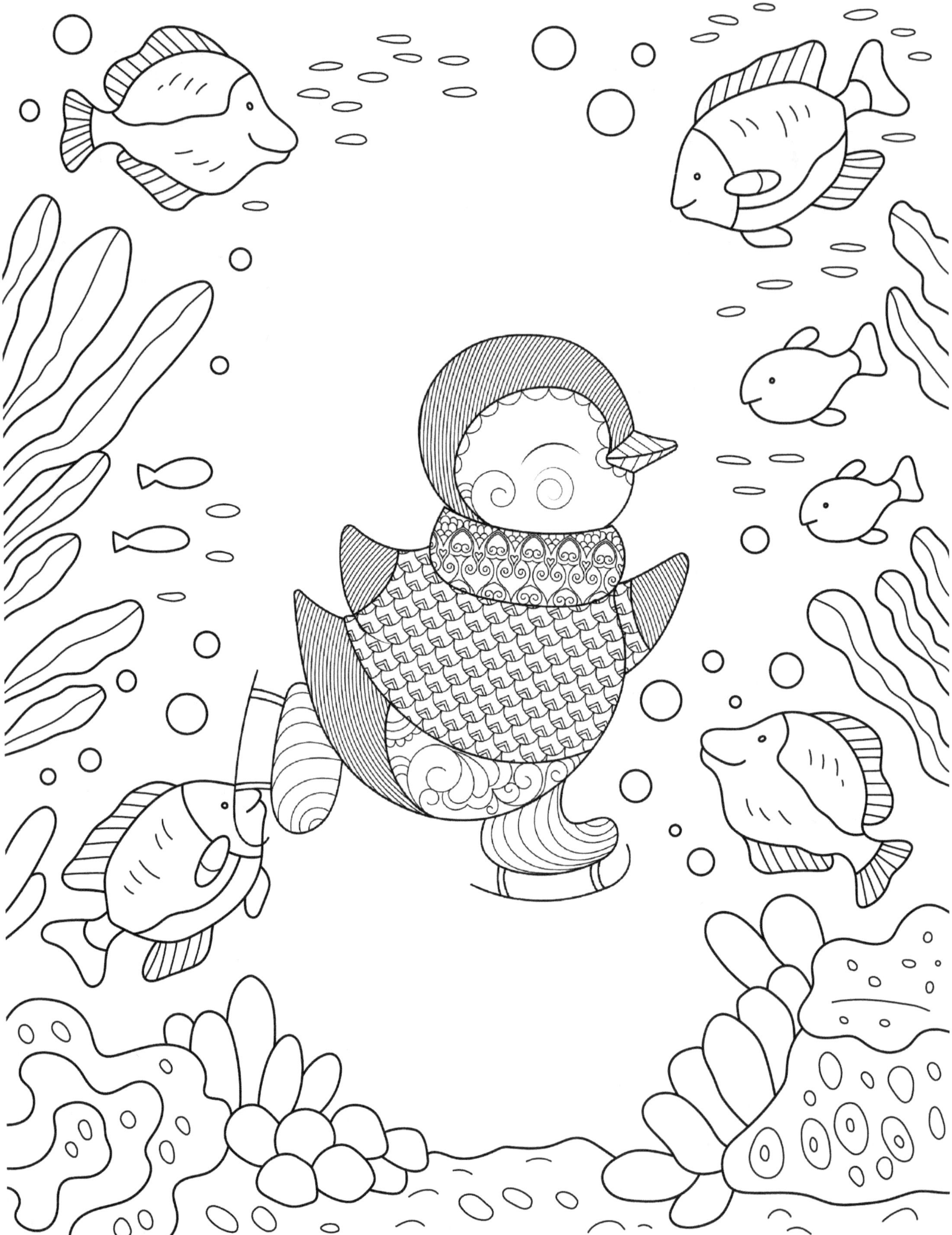

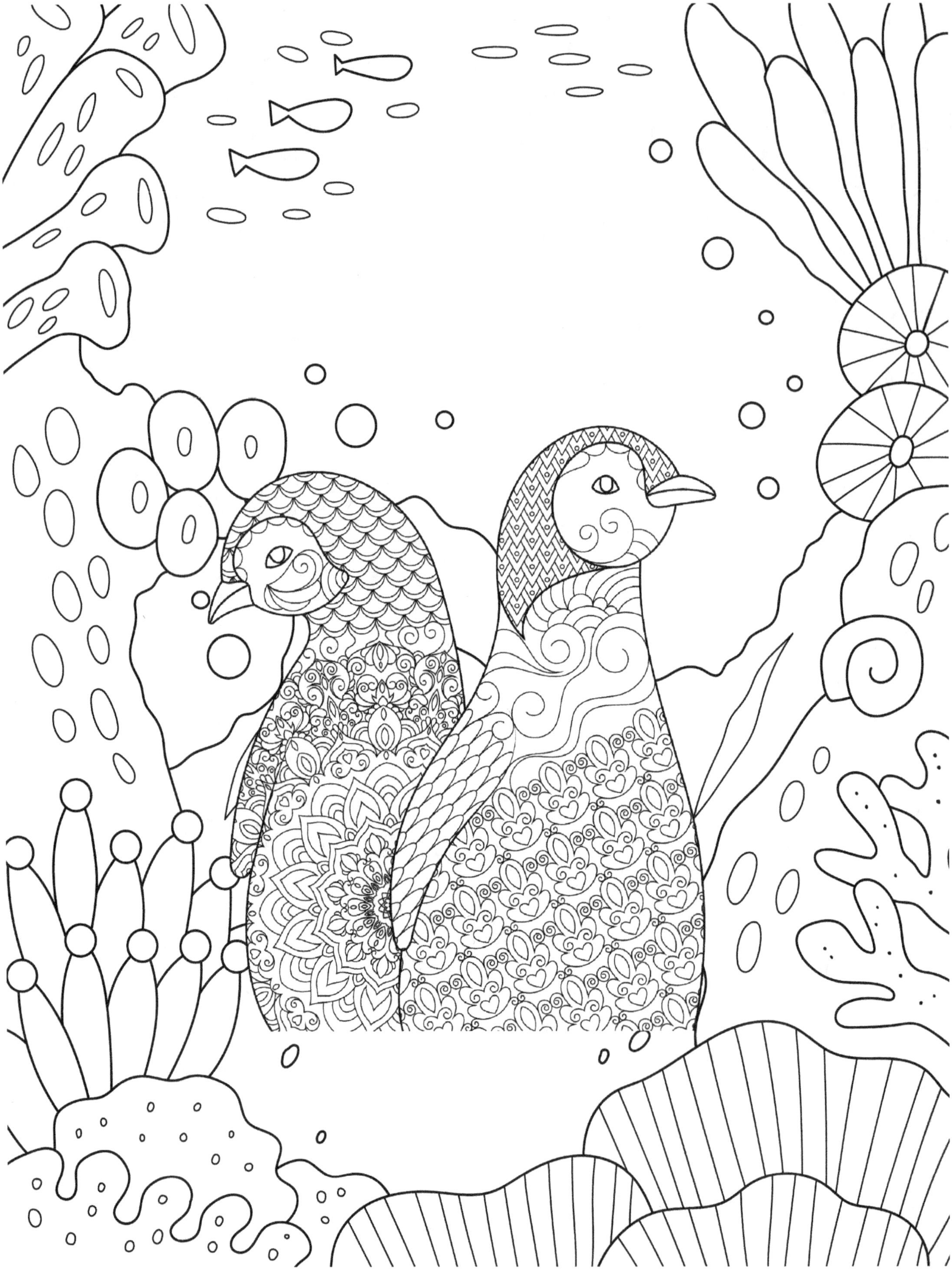

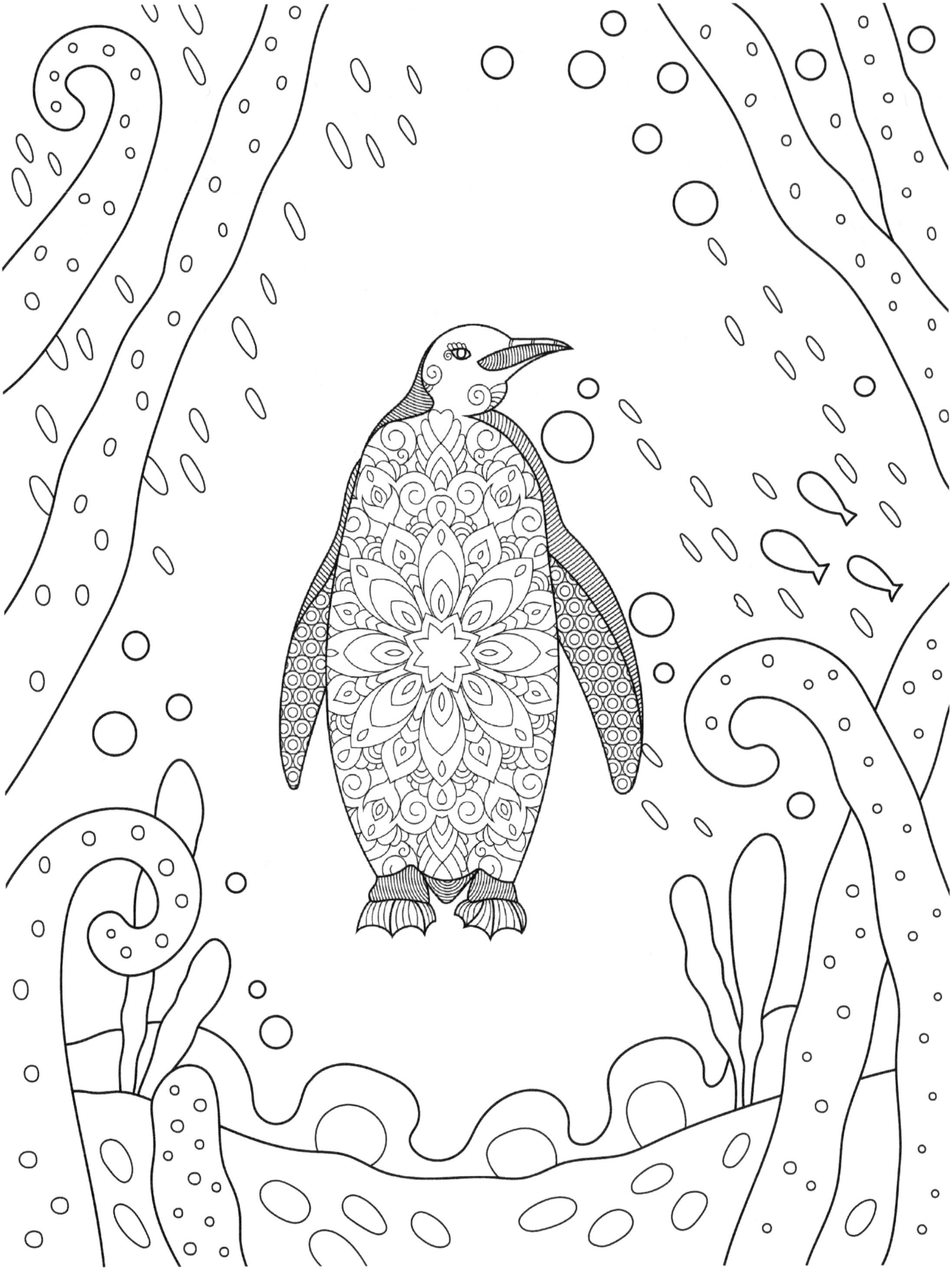

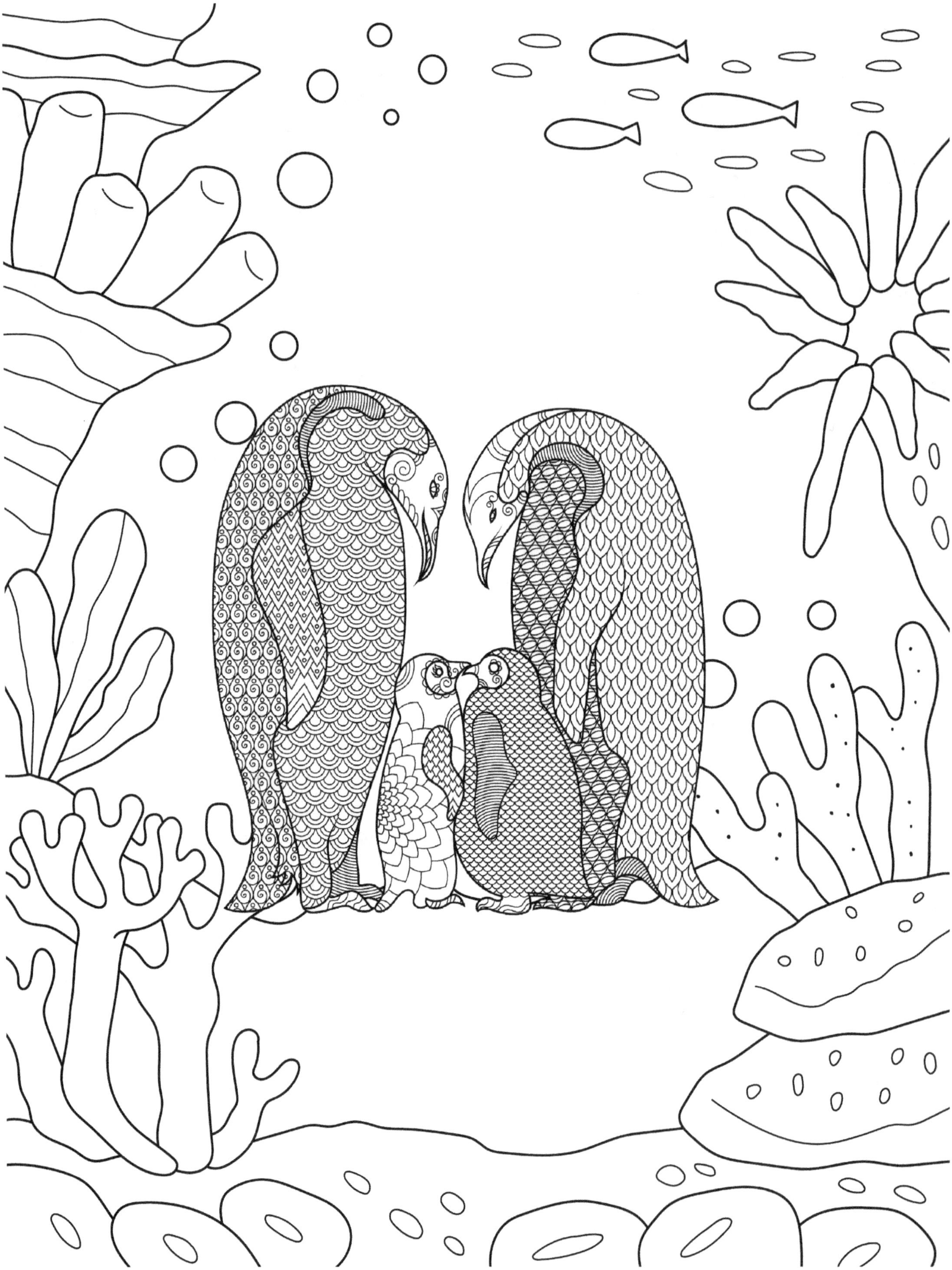

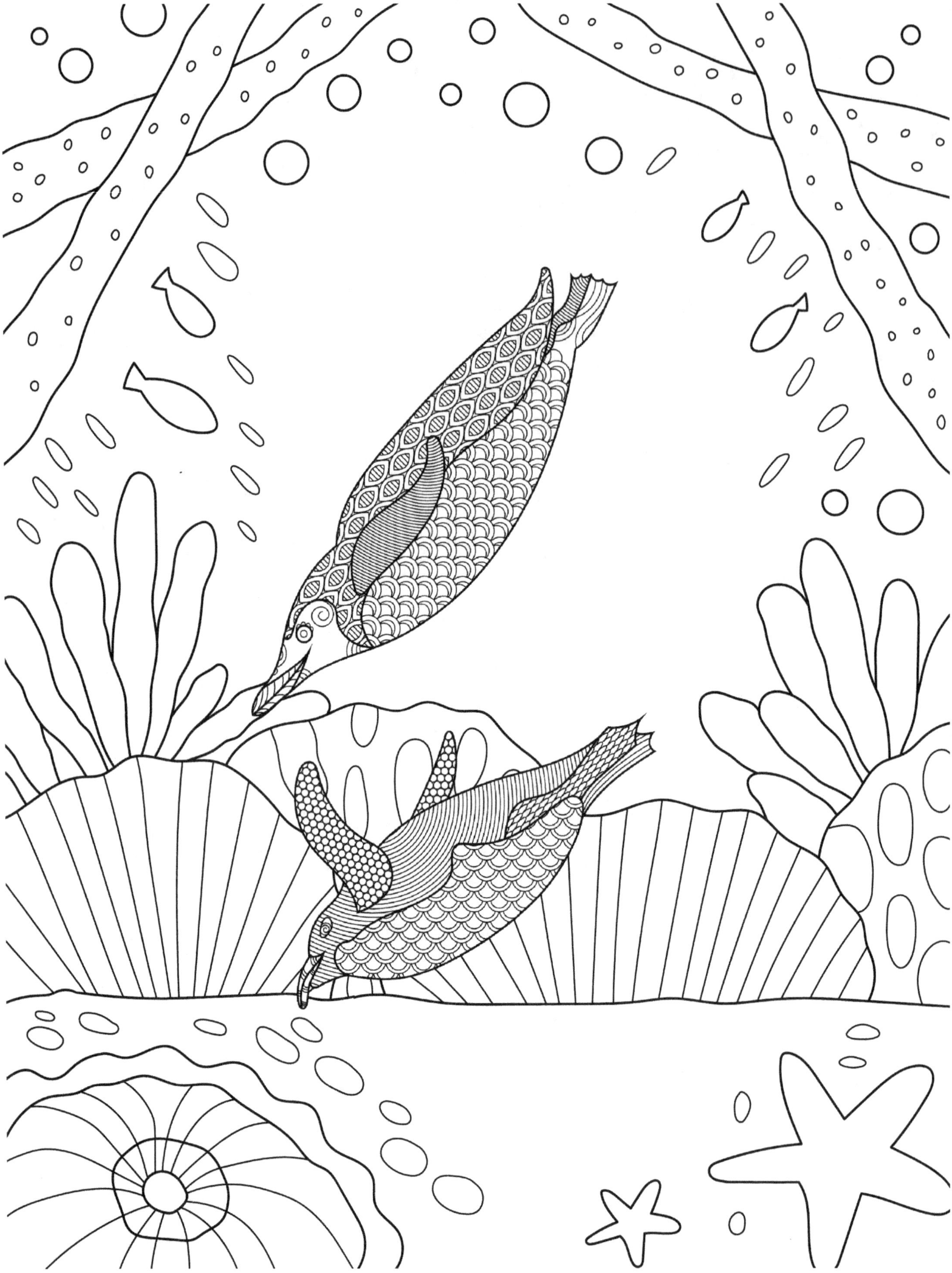

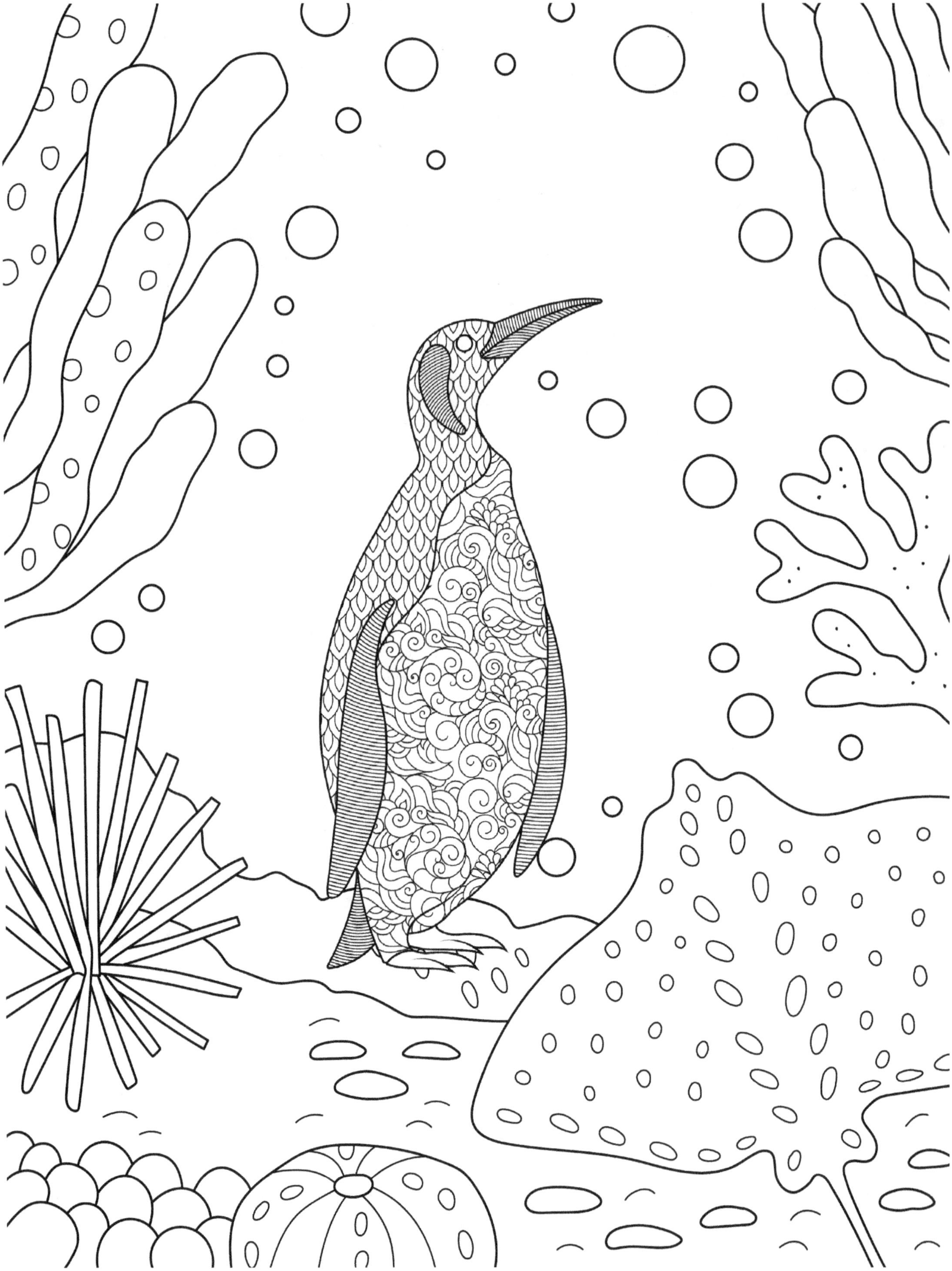

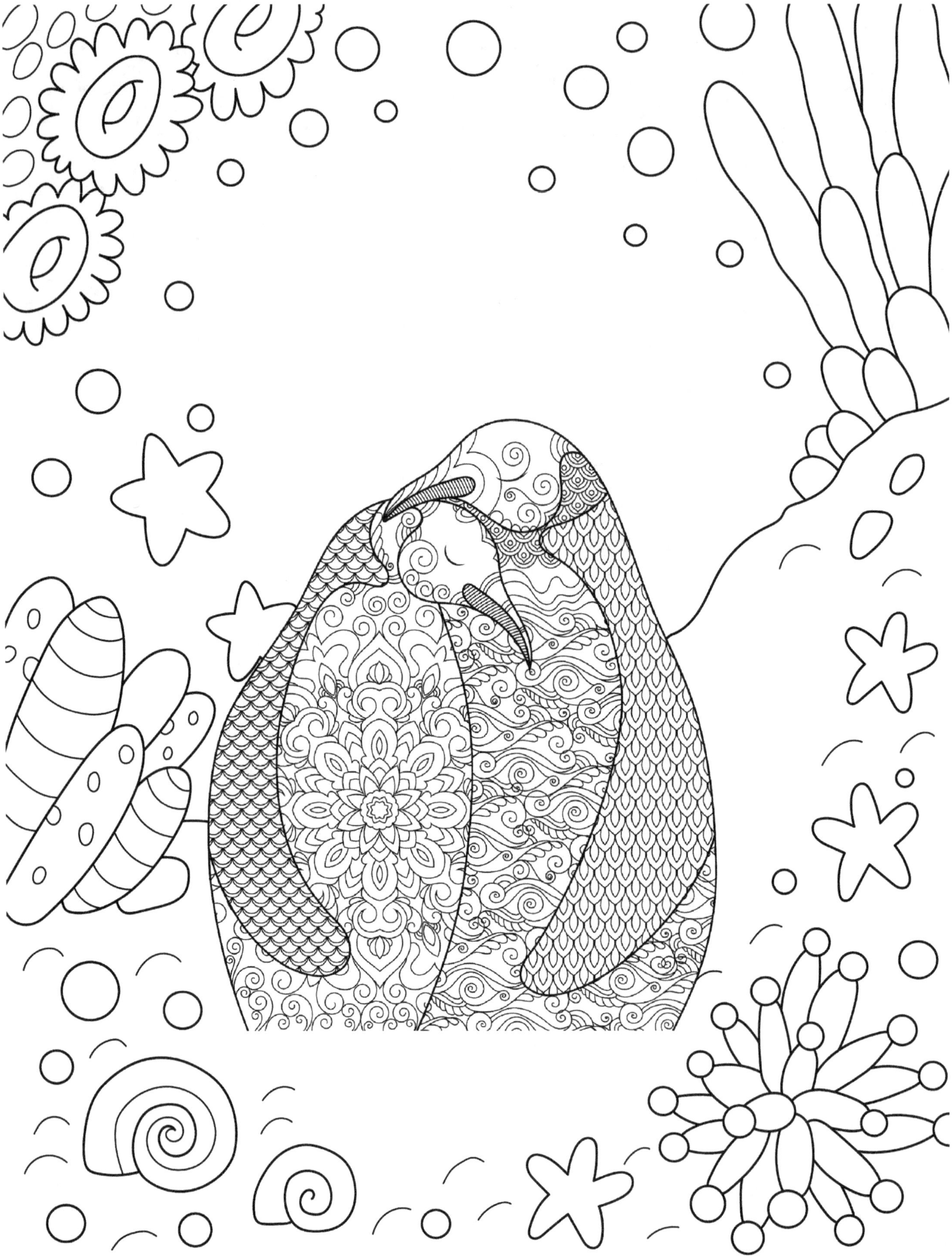

www.ingramcontent.com/pod-product-compliance
Lightning Source LLC
Chambersburg PA
CBHW082120220526
45472CB00009B/2249
* 9 7 9 8 4 8 6 4 9 8 6 0 2 *